Marisa Cruz

BEYOND PRISON THOUGHTS

BEYOND PRISON THOUGHTS

Lessons in listening and healing

M. Cruz

The German National Library lists this publication in the German National Bibliography; detailed bibliographic data is available online at http://dnb.dnb.de.

This memoir is based on the author's experiences. Some names, locations, and details have been changed to protect privacy. Dialogue and events have been recreated from memory.

Cover design by Julia and Matheo Carvalho Moebus.

Publisher: BoD · Books on Demand GmbH, Überseering 33, 22297 Hamburg, bod@bod.de
Print: Libri Plureos GmbH, Friedensallee 273, 22763 Hamburg
ISBN: 978-3-8192-7739-9

To my mum, who made me passionate about reading and believing, and to all other mums who keep the candle of love lighting.

"As human beings, our greatness lies not so much in being able to remake the world - that is the myth of the atomic age - as in being able to remake ourselves."

Mahatma Gandhi

Table of Contents

Prison isn't just a place—it's a world within a world, hidden behind walls yet deeply connected to society. When we think of prison, we picture towering concrete walls and heavy metal bars. But the truth is, prison is more than that. It's a thought. The prison we see with our eyes is merely a reflection of the one that exists in the mind. A single thought can set you free. A single thought can lock you in.

Most of us will never walk through the gates of a prison made of stone and steel, but many of us know what it feels like to be trapped—by fear, doubt, or the limits we place on ourselves. This book isn't about crime and punishment in the usual sense. It's about what I've learned from those who live behind bars—not just about them, but about all of us. About me. About you. I never set out to explore prison life. My journey into this hidden world began unexpectedly—through a deep sense of connection, compassion, and responsibility I couldn't ignore. I wasn't a criminologist, psychologist, or social worker. I was just someone who started listening. I listened to the stories of incarcerated women—stories of struggle, resilience, regret, and, most unexpectedly, hope.

What I found in these encounters challenged everything I thought I knew. I met people whose lives had been shaped by poverty, addiction, desperation, and circumstances they felt powerless to change. Some had made reckless choices; others had been manipulated or coerced. A few carried deep regret for their actions, while some still struggled to fully grasp the weight of what they had done. But beyond their convictions and sentences, they were human—complex, flawed, and searching for meaning, just like the rest of us.

This book is not a plea for sympathy, nor is it an argument against justice. It is an invitation to look beyond the labels—criminal, offender, prisoner—and see the person behind the crime. It is about dismantling the illusion that "good people" and "bad people" exist in neat, separate categories. And it is about confronting an uncomfortable truth: that under different circumstances, any of us could have ended up on the other side of the bars. By sharing these lessons, I hope to offer a perspective that is often overlooked: prisons don't just hold criminals—they hold stories. Stories that, if we truly listen, can teach us about resilience, redemption, and the power of change. If you choose to keep reading, I ask only this: approach these pages not with judgment, but with an open mind. Look deeper. Listen closely. There is wisdom in truth, and peace in understanding. Everything begins with a thought. And in many ways, we are our thoughts.

This is a book about lessons learned at the prison, but not in the prison.

INTRODUCTION
How It All Started

No, you don't have to be an offender to experience the harsh realities of prison. You can witness it through the eyes of those who live it every day. Why should you care? Well, you don't have to. But if you ever do, it might just change the way you see the world. It could challenge your assumptions, expand your perspective, and—perhaps most importantly—help you develop a deeper sense of empathy for people whose lives have been shaped by circumstances most of us will never fully understand. You might be wondering: What would drive someone with no background in social science or psychology—someone with a stable job, a fulfilling personal life, and an already packed schedule—to start visiting women in prison? Trust me, I've been asked that question more times than I can count.

And honestly? It depends on who's asking. At work, very few of my colleagues even know I volunteer at a jail. It's not something I bring up often—partly because it feels personal, but also because, well... it's not exactly the easiest topic to relate to over coffee.

But one day, during lunch, a coworker and I got into a conversation about—of all things—the complex chemistry behind refining cocaine. Yep, that's just what happens when chemists start talking! We can't help but analyze and theorize. What started as a purely technical discussion took an unexpected turn. I shared something I had learned from my time volunteering—that in some countries, the length of a prison sentence is influenced by the purity of the drug. The higher the purity, the harsher the sentence. So, when someone decides to smuggle drugs, such as cocaine across borders, they're not just committing a crime—they might also be unknowingly making their situation way worse if they don't know exactly what they're carrying. The purer the substance, the longer the punishment if they get caught.

It's wild to think that something that starts as a "natural" product—coca leaves—ends up being transformed into a dangerous cocktail of chemicals. For context, a single coca leaf contains only about 1% cocaine, and it takes roughly 140 kg of coca leaves just to produce one kilogram of coca paste. The world of drug trafficking is complex, dangerous, and often deadly—not just for those involved in production and smuggling, but for everyone touched by its ripple effects, from law enforcement to families and entire communities. It's a brutal, unforgiving business. And this is where the prison experience ties in.

The people caught up in this cycle aren't just "criminals"—many of them are victims of a system that offers little to no way out. Visiting women in jail has shown me just how layered these stories are. The path to incarceration isn't always as simple as it seems. Behind every conviction, there's a deeper story—one of survival, desperation, or circumstances beyond a person's control. It's a reminder that we're all part of a bigger picture. And sometimes, just being open to someone else's reality is enough to change the way we see the world.

But back to my colleague—he looked at me, surprised, and asked with a mix of curiosity and amusement, "Where the hell did you learn that?" I took a deep breath and explained that I visited South American women incarcerated in Germany for drug trafficking. His response was immediate: "Why would you do that? They got what they deserved. They're there for a reason." I was taken aback. Had he never heard of compassion? I paused, not just to put myself in his shoes, but to step into his mindset. What had shaped his perspective? His reaction wasn't uncommon but coming from someone I had always seen as kind and open-minded, it stung.

After a moment, I explained my perspective. Slowly, he began to understand, though he still cautioned me to be careful because "it could be dangerous." I thanked him for the concern and moved on. But the question lingered: What drives me to do this? If I said it was purely about following in Jesus' footsteps, that would be an oversimplification—lacking depth, maybe even sounding superficial. That's not the full picture.

My decision comes from something deeper—something beyond religious beliefs. It's a universal drive that exists in all of us: a pull toward justice, a desire to do the right thing, to care for and protect others. Some might call it instinct. But I believe it's more than that—it's an innate sense of shared humanity, something we are born with. And back to Jesus—I'm sure that's what he was trying to teach all along. Take a moment—just a moment—with an open mind and a peaceful heart. Think back to a time when you felt an inner call to help or protect someone. Maybe it was standing up for a classmate at school, offering a hand to a stranger struggling with their groceries, or simply sending a kind thought to someone facing an illness. We all have those moments, whether big or small—not that kindness can truly be measured anyway. Social media is filled with inspiring videos—on YouTube, TikTok, and beyond—of people jumping into action during emergencies: earthquakes, car accidents, natural disasters, or any moment where someone needs immediate help. And in those moments, no one stops to ask, "Does this person deserve to be helped? Have they made mistakes in the past?" It just happens. We just do it. Compassion takes over. We act instinctively, without hesitation, because deep down, we know it's the right thing to do. And if you think back to a moment like that in your own life, you'll probably remember the warmth it gave you—the quiet, unspoken joy of doing something good.

From the perspective of the person being helped, that kindness can ripple outward. It might even inspire them to pass it forward when they can. And just like that, without even realizing it, a circle of kindness is formed. This instinct to help isn't just a human trait—it extends to the animal kingdom as well. The ancient philosopher Pythagoras believed that animals experience the full range of emotions, including fear, joy, and compassion.

We see proof of this all the time—dogs comforting their humans after trauma, elephants mourning the loss of a friend, and animals showing deep, unspoken care for one another. These moments aren't calculated; they're pure. As Buddha might say, they are true acts of compassion. For me, though, there's another layer to this motivation. I currently live in Germany, near Frankfurt—a place many would consider safe. No slums, a strong social support system, and a good education structure. Of course, what counts as "good" education is up for debate, but that's a conversation for another time.

The point is, that I live in a stable and secure environment, at least in terms of crime. But it wasn't always this way for me. I grew up in the ghettos of São Paulo, one of the largest and most unforgiving cities in South America. My childhood—and even my early adult years—were shaped by the constant presence of crime, violence, and a sense of fear that dictated everyday life. It was an environment where survival often came before dreams, and safety was never guaranteed.

To be clear, this was about 40 years ago—things have improved a lot since then. But the experience left a mark, shaping how I see the world and, more importantly, how I see the people society often forgets. If you take the time to really look at the roots of crime and violence, you'll see a common thread weaving through it all: drugs. From solvents to marijuana, cocaine to amphetamines—people have always found ways to chase that high, to escape reality, or to numb the weight of their existence. And the drug trade? It's ruthless. It doesn't care who it destroys. It infects every level of society, from street corners to corporate boardrooms, leaving devastation in its wake. I saw it firsthand. Families ripped apart. Communities crumbling. Lives lost—some to addiction, some to violence, some to both. And the impact doesn't stop with the users or the dealers. It spreads like wildfire, pulling in parents, children, neighbors, employers— anyone close enough to get caught in the web. This is why I do what I do. I want to remind those who have been pulled into the world of drugs that they can choose again. That their past does not have to define them. Having witnessed the destruction caused by addiction in my own community and understanding the struggles of those trapped in the system, I feel a deep responsibility to do something—anything—to help.

To be clear, I don't see the women I visit in jail as criminals. I see them as people—human beings shaped by circumstances far beyond their control. Yes, they may have made wrong choices. But I refuse to believe that one wrong choice should determine their worth. In many cases, their stories have little to do with personal failure and everything to do with a system designed to keep them stuck. And that is what drives me to volunteer—to listen, to offer compassion, and to help these women find a path toward healing and redemption. It's about creating a space where they can reclaim their dignity, where their humanity is seen beyond their mistakes. And in doing so, I remind myself of the deeper connection we all share. Because in the end, it's not about who deserves help. It's about showing up for each other when it matters most. In the grand scheme of things, we are all part of the same story. And no matter how much we try to distance ourselves from the struggles of others, real change happens when we lean in—when we face the pain instead of turning away. Only then can we truly make a difference, opening a space for that pain to be acknowledged, healed, and, one day, released.

So if someone asked me why I wrote this book, I'd say I had three major goals. First, I hope the wild ups and downs, the real pain and tough stories in here, serve as a kind of wake-up call. Life can throw some heavy stuff at us—money problems, breakups, work stress—you name it. And when you're in the middle of it, it's easy to make a snap decision that only makes things worse. Especially if you're thinking about turning to drugs or getting into something illegal to escape. I hope these stories help you or someone you know pause and think twice before taking a path that's way harder to come back from.

Second, I want to speak to anyone who's ever looked at someone going through the justice system—facing charges, going to prison, or trying to rebuild after all that. It's so easy to judge. But here's the thing: we usually don't know the full story. People are more than their mistakes. So if you can't show compassion, that's okay—but at least try not to judge too fast. You never know how much a bit of kindness can shift someone's whole day—or life.

And third, if you've ever thought about getting more involved—whether it's helping underprivileged kids, homeless animals, protecting the environment, supporting people who are mentally or physically ill, or anything that's been tugging at your heart—this is your sign. Go for it. Take that first step. You might be surprised at how much it gives back to you and how strong it makes you feel when life gets rough. So yeah, that's the heart behind this book. It's not just stories— it's a little nudge, a bit of advice, and a whole lot of hope.

Because sometimes, all it takes is hearing that someone else made it through the storm to believe you can too.

CAUGHT BY ILLUSIONS

I remember those moments as if they happened yesterday. I saw things no child should have to see—lifeless bodies on the street, sudden bursts of gunfire, and people so consumed by drugs that they wandered aimlessly, like shadows of their former selves. But the most heartbreaking moment? The day I realized that someone I loved—a childhood friend—had been pulled into that same dark world. His nickname was Bingo. We grew up together in the same neighborhood, part of the same tight-knit kids' crew. Around the time we turned 12, I started noticing changes. He began skipping school, distancing himself from the playgrounds where we used to meet.

It was subtle at first, but soon it became clear—something was wrong. Bingo lived with his mom and three siblings. His mother worked tirelessly as a housekeeper in downtown São Paulo, doing everything she could to provide for them. They were the kind of family that always found reasons to smile, no matter how tough things got. His father? Gone. Left them all behind to chase a new life with a younger woman, abandoning not just his family but the mountain of debts he had accumulated. I never asked Bingo how he felt about it, but I could tell—his silence spoke volumes. One day, I decided to check in on him. I knocked on his door—most houses didn't have doorbells back then— and asked if he wanted to come outside and play. I also mentioned that I was worried since he had been missing school. And that's when it happened.

Instead of answering, Bingo flashed a wide grin and eagerly showed me his brand-new New Balance shoes, fresh clothes, and a brand-new electronic game. My stomach dropped. My heart sank. I didn't need to ask where it all came from. I already knew. I couldn't hold back. I had to ask, "How in the world did you afford all of this? Please don't tell me you're being used as a mule?" In Brazil, people who transport drugs—whether across borders or through airports—are commonly called "mules." Bingo just shrugged. "It's none of your business," he said, brushing me off. "It's an easy job. There's nothing to worry about. It's not as bad as it seems." I glanced over at his mother. She stood there, silent, her face etched with worry. She looked lost, overwhelmed, and completely powerless against the storm that was unfolding before her eyes. Desperation took over. I begged him to stop. "Please, before it's too late." He just smiled and told me not to worry.

I went home in tears, feeling utterly helpless. A few months passed. I tried reaching out to Bingo again, but he had disappeared. Then the news came: he had been caught by the police. Just like that, he was gone from my life. His family vanished overnight, likely fearing retaliation from the drug dealers. That was the first time I truly grasped how predictable these tragedies were. In countries where kids are pulled into drug trafficking at such a young age, the pattern is painfully clear—it all starts with skipping school. If it's so obvious, then why haven't we figured out how to stop it? Why does it keep happening?

Time moved on, but the cycle didn't break. Another friend, Nico, got caught in the same trap. He was about 16—quiet, introverted, never the type to run with the street crowd. But somewhere along the way, he started experimenting with drugs. Then came the so-called friends who convinced him to help them rob a gas station in a nearby neighborhood. "It'll be easy," they told him. "Like spreading butter on warm bread." They were wrong. The robbery turned into chaos. Someone inside managed to call the police. And by sheer bad luck, the ROTA—the most feared police force in São Paulo— was just around the corner. Nico ran. He sprinted through the streets, desperate to reach our neighborhood, to make it home, to find safety with his parents. But he never made it.

Somewhere along the way, exhausted and out of breath, he must have ducked into an abandoned construction site, hoping to disappear into the shadows. But ROTA officers had an uncanny ability to track people down—like bloodhounds sniffing out fear and sweat. ROTA was originally created in the 1970s to crush left-wing rebels during Brazil's military dictatorship. Decades later, their methods hadn't changed much. They still operated with ruthless efficiency. One of the officers spotted Nico, crouched behind a crumbling wall. And in São Paulo, when ROTA comes, they don't ask questions. They shoot first. Nico was shot dead just a few meters from his home. No warning. No second chances. No space for forgiveness.

It was one of the most painful experiences of my childhood.

It took years to process, to even begin to understand the weight of what had happened. His parents and older brother—once so warm, always greeting us with kindness—shut themselves inside their home for months. The grief was suffocating. Their house, once filled with laughter, became a place of silence and shadows. The whole neighborhood felt it. It was as if we were all holding our breath, waiting for the next tragedy. Because that was the real question lingering in every parent's mind: Who would be next? And I couldn't stop asking myself—how many more kids like Nico will never get the chance to choose again?

Why do so many families face this tragic fate in countries where drugs rule the streets? Nico's family wasn't struggling financially—by local standards, they were actually doing better than most of us. So why did he experiment with drugs? Why did he get involved in that robbery?

It wasn't about money. And that realization left me shaken. I had always assumed poverty was the main driver behind these choices. That was the narrative we were told, the explanation that made sense. But Nico didn't fit the statistic curve. He was an outlier. An outlier? That question haunted me. It forced me to reconsider everything I thought I knew. What really pushes someone to take that first step toward self-destruction? Was it peer pressure? A search for meaning? A silent, unspoken hopelessness? Or was it simply the desperate need to belong, to be seen? What I began to realize was that it wasn't just poverty trapping kids like Bingo and Nico in this cycle—it was something much deeper. A web of systemic issues, broken homes, artificial lives, and the absence of real support. Drugs, crime, and violence weren't just vices; they were coping mechanisms, escape routes, and ways to numb the pain or prove one's worth in a world that offered little else. And when you're surrounded by it every day, breaking free feels almost impossible. Almost.

Because we must believe—where there is a will, there is a way. You have to hope for a miracle. That was when I truly began to understand—the problem is bigger than any one person or family. It's systemic. It infects entire communities, sinking its roots so deep that breaking free seems impossible. But that's exactly why we can't afford to give up. That understanding is what keeps so many of us going—fighting to break the cycle, even if we can only save one life at a time. I may not have all the answers. But I do know this: as long as there are more Bingos and Nico's out there, we have a responsibility to keep trying.

NAVIGATING DANGERS

Growing up near the ghettos of a massive city is an experience most people can't even begin to imagine. And sometimes, it's worse than you'd think. I was in fourth grade, attending a primary school about three kilometers from home. Every day, I walked to school— through streets where danger lurked in the corners, where violence was a daily reality, and where survival meant keeping your head down and your senses sharp. The worst part of my journey was a narrow alleyway, called a *viela* in Brazilian Portuguese. It stretched uphill, winding between tightly packed houses. And every single day, as I approached that alley, my heart pounded. That *viela* was a gamble. I never knew what was waiting around the bend. The curve in the alley meant I couldn't see ahead, couldn't anticipate what—or who—was on the other side.

So I did the only thing I could: I prayed for protection. I sang to distract myself. And I walked forward, hoping that today wouldn't be the day I ran into something I couldn't escape. Then, one day, it happened—the day of panic. As I turned the corner, humming to myself, I froze. A man lay on the ground. Motionless. Shot dead.

He was probably around 30, with short, curly black hair, dressed well—too well for this alley. Beside him, a small package rested on the ground. I couldn't process it fast enough. My breath caught in my throat. My heart pounded. Was the gunman still nearby? Was I next? Panic took over. My legs moved before my brain could think. I ran. School was closer than home, so I sprinted in that direction, my feet barely touching the ground. The world blurred past me.

My only thought was: get away, get away, get away. Halfway there, I spotted a man walking on the other side of the street. I must have looked like a ghost—wild-eyed, desperate, shaking. I veered toward him, crying, barely able to speak. "I just saw—" My words tumbled out. "A dead man. Shot. Please. Call the police." He stiffened.

His face mirrored my fear. Then, after a pause, he muttered, "Don't worry. I'll take care of it." But I didn't wait to see if he would. I just ran. By the time I reached school, I was still in shock. My body was there, but my mind was trapped back in that *viela*, standing over that lifeless body. I couldn't speak. Couldn't think. My teacher noticed something was off. That was when I broke. The tears came, and I begged to go home. Looking back, I realize that was a bold move. Schools in São Paulo were strict—punishment-based learning was the norm. Once, I had to stand behind the classroom door for a full hour just to be a few seconds late after lunch break. But none of that mattered now. I was terrified. I kept asking myself: Was that real? Did I just see that? Or was this all some kind of nightmare?

The teacher, clearly caught off guard by my sudden request, took a deep breath and asked me to calm down. "Just give me a good reason," she said. But at that moment, all I could think about was getting home— running straight into my mother's arms, where I knew I'd feel safe again.

In a moment of desperation, the words just spilled out: "My uncle was shot dead at that corner of the alleyway." She froze, her expression shifting from shock to sympathy. "Oh, my dear... I'm so sorry," she murmured. She didn't press me for details, didn't make me stay. She just let me go. I took the long way home, deliberately avoiding that alley. Even from a distance, I could see the flashing lights, and the crowd of police and paramedics clustered around the crime scene. I didn't need to get any closer. I already knew how these things played out. In our neighborhood, deaths like this were almost always tied to gang disputes. The full story behind that man's death? I'll probably never know. But the memory of that day—the sight, the fear, the way it made my stomach twist—has never left me. It changed me. It shaped how I see the world, and how I understand the harsh realities of life in places like the one where I grew up.

After that, my mom didn't hesitate. She started looking for another school, somewhere safer, somewhere with better opportunities. She wanted me to have a way out. I was always pretty good in school— curious, eager to learn, and constantly buried in books.

My mom noticed I needed more of a challenge, so she made a bold move: she transferred me to a school in another town, one known for being more demanding.

The only downside? I had to take a packed bus every day. And just like that, in the 5th grade, I found myself in a completely new environment. Fitting in wasn't exactly a struggle, but I often felt like a fish out of water. My new school was in Santo André, a town known for its wealthier residents, while I came from a neighborhood where crime was a daily reality.

The contrast was obvious. None of my new school friends ever wanted to visit me—they were afraid of what they'd heard about my area. Sometimes, they'd ask ridiculous questions, like if I could hear gunshots from my house or if I had drug dealers in my family. I'd laugh it off, but deep down, it stung. As the years passed, the "new" school wasn't new anymore. By the time I hit 8th grade, I had my circle of friends, my rhythm, and a clearer sense of where I fit in.

That's when I met Tata. Tata was the kind of person who didn't just walk into a room—she owned it. People followed her like she was some kind of celebrity. With her bright red hair, trendy outfits, and natural confidence, she always seemed to know what was happening before anyone else did. But what really set her apart? She was an absolute beast at sports. In dodgeball, if Tata's ball hit you, you felt it for days.

Despite her popularity, I noticed she struggled in certain subjects—especially Math and English. One day, I saw her stuck on a math problem, and without thinking twice, I offered to help. She shot me a look that said, How dare you? —but then, something shifted. She realized I wasn't trying to show off; I genuinely wanted to help. That was the moment everything changed. From that day on, we became close friends. Every now and then, Tata would invite me over to her house after school. She didn't live far, and although her home was modest, her father ran a *barraca de frutas* (fruit stand) that was the place to be. It wasn't just a spot to buy fruit—it was a neighborhood hotspot, buzzing with life. At night, young people gathered around, chatting and laughing under the streetlights. I would have loved to experience that more, but my mom rarely let me go out after dark.

Tata had a sister in her twenties who always seemed weighed down by something, her face a mix of sadness and anger. One day, Tata confided in me—her sister's husband had been sentenced to jail for stealing cars. Then, out of nowhere, Tata stopped coming to school. Days passed, and she was still absent. I asked around, but no one gave me a clear answer. A classmate who knew her family simply said they were going through some trouble—and left it at that. About a week later, Tata finally showed up—but not like before. She didn't stroll in with her usual confidence. Instead, she arrived after the school day had already started, knocking on our classroom door. "Can I talk to her for a second?", pointing at me she asked the teacher, her voice softer than usual. The teacher nodded kindly, and we stepped into the hallway.

She looked... different. The girl who always lit up the room now seemed drained, as the weight of the world had settled on her shoulders. Her eyes were tired, her expression heavy with something unspoken. Seeing her like that almost made me tear up. I held her gaze, searching for the strong, fearless friend who had always inspired me. The moment the classroom door clicked shut behind us, she took a deep breath and got straight to the point. Her voice was strained as she asked, "Do you remember that my brother-in-law is in jail?" I nodded, my heart pounding, waiting for whatever came next. What she told me was shocking. Her sister—madly in love with her imprisoned husband and devastated by his fate—had attempted to break him out. She had tried to smuggle a gun into the prison. Now, she was locked up too.

Their father had completely lost it, overwhelmed by the situation, and Tata was caught in the chaos. She looked at me, hesitation in her eyes, before finally asking, "Could you bring me the lessons from school for the next few weeks?" I froze. On one hand, I wanted to help my friend—of course, I did. But at the same time, I knew my mom would never approve of me getting involved with a family facing criminal charges. If she found out, I'd be in serious trouble.

That night, I couldn't sleep. My mind kept spinning, torn between two choices: do the right thing and help my friend, or stay out of it and protect myself. In the end, I made my decision. I would help her. But I wouldn't tell my mom. The situation was overwhelming, and it became a turning point for both Tata and me. We were just teenagers, but suddenly, life wasn't about schoolwork and gossip anymore—we were face-to-face with the kind of harsh realities that forced us to grow up fast. That moment changed me. It made me realize how fragile life is, how quickly things can spiral out of control, and how, even in the middle of chaos, the choices we make define who we become.

Those days were challenging, but they also gave me some unforgettable adventures—experiences that, in many ways, shaped the person I am today. Tata, despite everything she was going through, inspired me. She had this confidence, this fearlessness that rubbed off on me. When I arrived at her house, we didn't waste time. First, we tackled the schoolwork—I'd go over the lessons of the day with her. Then, I'd help restock the fruit stand, arranging bananas, mangoes, and pineapples like we were running some kind of art display.

One time, as we worked, she casually pointed to a hidden compartment under the stand. "That's where we keep the guns," she said. I froze. It was the first time I had ever seen a gun up close. My stomach twisted as I stared at the cold metal. It was terrifying to think how something so small could take a life in seconds. Still, life around the fruit stand had its fun moments too.

A couple of times, I got to tag along when Tata had to restock missing products. The real kicker? Even though you had to be 18 to drive in Brazil, her dad let her drive their old Volkswagen Transporter Type 2. And wow— she drove like she was in a high-speed chase. We'd hop into that car, and zip through the streets like maniacs, wind in our hair, music blasting. For those brief moments, nothing else mattered. We weren't thinking about her sister, the guns, or the weight of the world on our shoulders. We were just two teenagers, wild and free. And it felt amazing.

Then another turning point came. It was at her fruit stand that I met a sweet guy with whom I had some fun times. His name was Chris. He had a red Kawasaki ninja motorcycle. First, we started exchanging looks, and when I saw, I was riding that motorcycle at high speed on the roads hugging him from behind as tight as I could. Oh boy, if my mom had ever caught me! I was around 14 years old and he was in his 20's. Although we had no sex he kind of awoke my interest on the topic.

One day, Tata asked me to chat a bit about him. It seemed like she did not know where to start the conversation. I went ahead to help her out and said "Big sister jump into the topic. What do you want to tell me?". She laughed joyously and started asking me about my feelings about him, what I knew about him, and so forth. As the conversation developed, she found the courage or the right time to ask me to go slowly and be careful about him. She carefully found words to tell me that he was involved in robbery himself or how I imagined he was able to ride that expensive motorcycle. I got really confused and could not believe such a sweet and hot beauty could be involved in a robbery of any kind. After a moment of denial, I understood she wanted to warn me. I went home feeling... off. Sad. Like the whole world had suddenly stopped making sense. Why do people meet just to end up disappointing each other? Why did he choose that path? Could I change his mind before it was too late? Would he even listen to me, or was it better to pretend I didn't know anything?

My mind wouldn't stop spinning. In the end, I decided not to see him that week. It was harder than I thought. My appetite vanished. I had no energy, no motivation for anything. And then, something strange happened. For three nights in a row, I dreamed about him. Every time, it was the same—Chris standing there, smiling, waving goodbye. I woke up each morning feeling unsettled. Was he trying to tell me something? What did those dreams mean?

That weekend, still lost in my thoughts, I went to the beach with my oldest sister and my niece. The salty air, the crashing waves—I hoped it would clear my mind. That night, we decided to hop on one of those little street trains meant for kids—nothing serious, just a fun, silly ride to see more of the town. The kind of thing you do when you're just looking for lighthearted entertainment. At some point, the train had to stop because of traffic. I turned my head absentmindedly— and then, out of nowhere, a motorcycle appeared. And I swear it was him. A jolt of recognition shot through me. My breath caught. Our eyes locked, and for that split second, everything else disappeared. The street noise, the people, the lights—it all faded. And that smile on his face? It made me want to jump off the train and run straight into his arms. But just as quickly as it happened, it was over. The moment slipped away, swallowed by the chaos of the city.

Night had fallen, and the streets were packed with cars, and people rushing in every direction. I blinked, trying to make sense of it. Was it really him? Was it just a coincidence? I kept replaying that moment in my mind, over and over, certain it was real—yet completely unable to explain it. I started to get angry, imagining the worst. Maybe he was at the beach—with another girl. Or maybe he was just out with his friends, laughing, having the time of his life... without me. My mind wouldn't stop spinning, running wild with possibilities. And the more I thought about it, the more I convinced myself he was doing something reckless—something that would only make everything worse.

The next day, I went to school, still feeling uneasy. Still trying to make sense of what I had seen. Still missing him. Then, as if on cue, my friend walked up to me. Her face was different—serious, almost too serious. My stomach tightened. "Have you heard what happened this weekend?" she asked. My heart skipped. A cold wave of dread washed over me. "No..." I said my voice barely above a whisper. She hesitated, then dropped the words that hit me like a brick: "Chris was killed Saturday night. During a bank robbery." Chris's gang had been planning to blow up an ATM machine. He was supposed to be the getaway driver. But the police had already been tipped off. They were waiting, ready. There was no way out. The shooting started. Chaos erupted. And Chris—still in his car—never made it out. Only one of the four gang members survived. He was the one who told the story.

I was in shock. This couldn't be real. It didn't make sense. I had seen him. I knew I had. My mind kept looping back to that moment on the street—his eyes, his smile. How could it have been him... but not him? Tata confirmed the news with a heavy heart. My own heart felt like it had shattered into pieces. I could barely breathe. The tears came fast before I could even process them. If only I had known. If only I had the chance to talk to him one last time. Maybe I could have said something—anything—to make him stop. But it was too late. And the worst part? We never even got to say goodbye.

Years passed, but that moment never left me. I found myself wondering—hoping, even—that maybe, just maybe, he knew how deeply I would grieve for him. Maybe that's why he appeared in my dreams, trying to comfort me, sending me a silent message that everything would be okay. And now, looking back, I wonder... was he, in some strange way, trying to tell me he was at peace? That it was his way of helping me heal, even when I couldn't understand it at the time? Who knows...

All those experiences shaped me into someone who was fearless and unimpressed by adversity. By the time I hit my late teenage years, I was diving headfirst into the world of discos, meeting people from all walks of life. My closest friends? Mostly boys who grew up in tough conditions, many of them from the slums near my home. Back then, there were no smartphones. If I wanted to hang out, I didn't text—I just walked straight into the heart of the slums to find them. To my family, this was borderline insanity. In their minds, slums equaled danger, crime, and trouble. But here's the thing—we knew that most of the people living there were some of the most honest, hardworking individuals I'd ever met. They weren't criminals; they just couldn't afford anything better. The real problem was that criminals knew how to use that to their advantage. They hid among the crowd, blending into the maze of tiny streets and makeshift homes, disappearing into the chaos. No street names. No real addresses. Just a place where everyone knew each other, and yet, anonymity was always an option.

But me? I never thought twice about walking through the slums, smiling, and greeting everyone like I belonged there. And in a way, I did. The people were used to me, and I was used to them. It felt like home—chaotic, gritty, but familiar. I remember one time, a friend invited me over to his place in the slum. It was raining, and he didn't want me standing outside getting drenched while he got ready. So, I stepped inside. And just like that, I entered another world—one that was both humbling and heartbreaking. The walls were thin, weathered wood, patched together with gaps so wide you could see the outside. The ceiling? Just a few flimsy planks nailed in place, barely holding up. And when it rained? Oh, it didn't just rain outside—it rained inside too. I stood there watching as water trickled down the walls, pooling in the corners, soaking everything in its path. Beds, furniture, clothes—nothing was spared. The air was thick with the damp, musty smell of mildew. And the floor? No tiles, no concrete. Just dirt. Uneven and rough, like the ground had been cleared but never properly finished.

It was a different reality—one I thought I knew but stepping inside made me realize how little I actually understood. The bedroom and kitchen were one and the same—a cramped space shared by five adults and a small child. Privacy? Nonexistent. Hygiene? A daily battle. And the air carried a heavy sense of struggle, like an invisible weight pressing down on everything. And the bathroom? Forget about it. A public latrine is shared with the entire neighborhood. I tried to play it cool, to act like it didn't shake me. The last thing I wanted was to make my friend feel embarrassed about his living situation. But inside? It hit me hard. This was the raw, unfiltered side of life—the side people don't talk about and don't want to see. And I was standing right in the middle of it. I never really told anyone about it. Not because I didn't care, but because I didn't even know how to put it into words. That was life in the slums near my home back then—a mix of joy and struggle, survival and hope. But things have changed.

Over the years, the slums have transformed. What was once a maze of wood and tin is slowly being replaced with brick houses, giving families a shot at a more stable, secure life. Progress is happening, even if it moves at a snail's pace. It feels like the people in those slums are finally being seen, finally getting some recognition for their resilience. Unfortunately, not everywhere in Brazil.

Life went on. I grew older and eventually became a teacher. For a couple of years, I taught high school chemistry at a public school near my town. It was a night class—crowded, with about 35 students, all young and full of energy. The school was located near a hot spot—an area where violence and drug trafficking were a part of everyday life. It was a tough environment, but I was determined to make a difference. One evening, since I was still new to the school, a kind student approached me before class. He seemed calm, but there was something serious in his expression. "Class has to be dismissed earlier today," he said. I frowned. "Why is that?"

Without hesitation, he replied, "Because the gangs have announced a dispute." I thanked him, though I couldn't understand why it should affect our class. So, I simply continued teaching. Then—boom! Loud fireworks exploded outside.

Before I could react, my students were already packing up and heading for the door, like it was the most natural thing in the world. Confused, I called out, "Wait! Where is everyone going?" The same boy who had warned me earlier turned back and said urgently, "That's the signal. They're warning the community to clear the streets and go home."

Still puzzled, I rushed to the principal's office for an explanation. He barely looked surprised. "That's the unofficial official warning system," he said calmly. "The drug dealer gangs use it to tell people to get off the streets before things get messy." Then, almost as an afterthought, he added, "You should go home too. You don't want to be caught in the middle of what's coming."

The truth was, the drug gangs didn't want civilians tangled up in their disputes. More attention meant more police presence—something they desperately wanted to avoid. So, in their own way, they had created a simple yet effective warning system. And like everyone else, I had to learn to listen.

Days passed, and I got used to the fireworks—no longer a sign of celebration, but a signal of life and death. One day, I noticed one of my best students had been missing class a lot. When she did show up, her eyes were swollen from crying, always surrounded by a small group of girls, whispering, and comforting her. I waited for the right moment before gently asking if there was anything I could do to help. She hesitated for a moment, then finally opened up. She had a violent ex-boyfriend— one who was stalking her, threatening to kill her. I felt my stomach drop. "Do your parents know?" I asked. She sighed, shaking her head. "They don't care. They warned me from the start that he wasn't worth it. So now, they say it's my problem." I couldn't believe what I was hearing.

I went straight to the school principal, hoping he'd step in. But all he did was shrug. "Do you think I'm crazy enough to risk my life getting involved in all the problems these kids have?" That was it. No concern, no action. Just self-preservation. Fair enough, I thought bitterly.

You wouldn't believe it, but one day, that boy actually showed up outside the school—yelling Linda's name at the top of his lungs. And guess what? It happened right in the middle of my class. Students shot up from their seats, craning their necks to peek through the windows.

Their faces weren't just curious—they were afraid. A few of them started whispering, saying they knew exactly who he was. Apparently, he used to be a student there... before getting caught by the police. Multiple times.

By the time class ended, Linda was a wreck. Her hands were shaking, and she kept glancing toward the door like a deer ready to bolt. I didn't even have to ask—I knew she was terrified to leave. "I'll walk you to the bus stop," I told her. And just as we expected, there he was. Coming straight toward us. Something about his walk was off—slow, unsteady. His eyes were wild, unfocused. It didn't take a genius to figure out he was under the influence of something A handsome 16-year-old boy—on the verge of ruining his life... or maybe even mine. I took a step forward, putting myself between him and Linda. My heart pounded, but I kept my voice steady. "Can I introduce myself?" I said, looking him right in the eye. "I'm Linda's chemistry teacher." He didn't care. "I don't give a shit," he spat, yanking Linda's arm violently. That was it—I stepped in. Placing a firm hand on his shoulder, I locked eyes with him and spoke with authority. "Do you realize you're scaring her with your mess? Can't you just give both yourself and her a break?" He froze, staring at me like I'd just spoken a language he didn't understand. So I kept going. "I know where I grew up. And if you're trying to intimidate me with your little act, be my guest. But listen—Linda is a great student. She has a future. And I bet you do too, if you stop wasting your life on nonsense. Sooner or later, you're gonna regret this. Why not choose differently now? Shock people with your strength, not your weakness."

For a second, he just stood there. Then, slowly, his grip on Linda's arm loosened. He didn't say a word. Just turned and walked away, deep in thought. I never heard about him again after that. As for Linda? She finished high school. And she did it successfully.

I look back on those days with a strange mix of nostalgia and awe. The people I met, the struggles I witnessed—they didn't just show me hardship; they taught me about strength, about resilience, about the kind of unbreakable spirit that refuses to be crushed. And you know what? As rough as the slums could be, they were also where I found some of the most real, unfiltered, ride-or-die friendships of my life. Now, I know what you're thinking—living in the troubled areas of São Paulo must have been terrifying, right? But honestly? Not at all. In fact, some of the best stories of my life happened right there.

Like this one time... There I was, waiting in line for a telephone booth—because, yep, having a landline at home was a luxury back then—when I accidentally became an audience member in a live soap opera. A woman, clearly at the breaking point, was on the phone with her partner. And let me tell you, she was not holding back. From what we all (unintentionally) gathered while waiting our turn, she had just found out that he had been cheating on her... with her best friend. In their own home. Oof.

You could feel the tension in the air. At that moment, the phone booth wasn't just a phone booth anymore—it was a stage, and we were all glued to the drama, waiting to see how it would unfold. As the argument escalated, so did the audience. At first, it was just a few curious glances, but soon, people started gathering—drawn in by the drama unfolding right in front of them. What had begun as a private fight had now turned into a full-blown public spectacle. And the yelling woman? She was too caught up in the heat of the moment to realize she'd just become the star of the show.

The crowd, like an eager theater audience, didn't hold back. They jumped in with unsolicited advice, passionately debating what she should do next. "She needs to leave him!" someone shouted. "No, no! Don't let him off that easy!" another argued. At this point, people weren't just watching—they were invested. Fully locked in. The energy around the phone booth was electric. With every heated word she threw into the receiver, the crowd reacted, like a live studio audience hanging onto every twist and turn. And before long, sides were forming. Some leaned in, whispering urgent advice, telling her she deserved better. Others nodded knowingly like they'd seen this movie before and already knew how it should end.

The moment stretched—10, 15, 20 minutes. An eternity. Normally, people would be banging on the booth, yelling at her to hurry up. But not today. Today, everyone was in it, wrapped up in the raw, messy, real drama playing out before them. Finally, the moment arrived. She took a deep breath, squared her shoulders, and said the words: "It's over." Boom. Done. And then—

chaos. The crowd erupted like a stadium after a winning goal. This wasn't just polite applause—it was a full-blown celebration. People were cheering, whistling, shouting over each other: "Go, girl! You don't need that loser!" "Kick him out of your house!"

"You deserve better!" It was like a scene straight out of a movie—the one where the underdog finally stands up for themselves, and the whole world rallies behind them. She stood there, frozen. Wait... had they been listening to the whole time? A wave of disbelief washed over her, quickly followed by something else. Something unexpected. Power. The validation from complete strangers hit differently. It wasn't just support—it was fuel.

She wiped her tears, stood a little taller, and with each step away, she felt lighter. Stronger. By the time she turned the corner, she wasn't the woman who had just been dumped. She was the woman who had just reclaimed her power.

That's São Paulo for you. A city that doesn't just watch from the sidelines—it jumps in, cheers you on, lifts you up. The energy here isn't just electric; it's alive. And in moments like these, you realize—it's got your back.

Now, don't get me wrong. Not every part of São Paulo is marked by crime. In fact, plenty of neighborhoods are peaceful and safe. And if there's one thing that truly stands out, it's the people. The warmth, the openness— it's unmatched. I've lived in and visited many places, but São Paulo? The people here make you feel like you belong. You could be walking down the street, and before you know it, you're deep in conversation with a total stranger—like you've been friends forever. The city never sleeps. There's always a buzz, an energy in the air. People are constantly interacting, sharing, and helping—giving whatever they can, no matter how little they have. It's just how things are here. And honestly? It's kind of wonderful.

RAISED BY THE FIGHTERS

There's something about the sense of community and openness in my old neighborhood that I'll always cherish. Every time I go back, it feels like a homecoming in the best way possible. Growing up in a poor neighborhood in the east zone of São Paulo wasn't always easy, but it shaped me. It gave me strength, resilience, and the kind of tough skin you don't just learn—you earn.

Little did I know, those lessons would prepare me for challenges I never even saw coming. Fast forward to one of my previous jobs at a major chemical company in Germany. Suddenly, I was jet-setting solo across the globe for business—Mexico, Italy, Russia, Turkey, England... you name it. Alone, a woman? You'd think that kind of travel might be intimidating, right? But honestly? I never felt unsafe and never doubted myself. Because when you grow up in an environment that teaches you how to stand your ground, you carry that confidence with you wherever you go. During my time in the USA, I attended a one-week Chemical Catalysis workshop at the University of Michigan in Detroit.

After landing, I picked up my rental car, drove to the hotel, and settled in. That night, I felt like going out. I've always loved theater, so I thought—why not catch a play? I had just finished reading *the five people you meet in Heaven* by Mitch Albom, and it had left a deep impression on me. To my delight, I discovered that a play by the same author was being performed that very night in Michigan. If memory serves me right, it was his comedy *And the Winner Is.*

As I was getting ready, a friendly front desk worker noticed and asked if I needed directions or maybe a restaurant recommendation. I told him I was heading to a theater a few miles away. His reaction? Pure shock. His eyes widened as he leaned in, lowering his voice like he was about to tell me a dark secret. "Uh... I wouldn't do that if I were you," he said, looking genuinely concerned. "Detroit at night can be dangerous, especially if you don't know the safe areas. You could get into real trouble." I listened carefully, nodding along. Then, with a casual shrug, I added, "I come from São Paulo." There was a beat of silence. And then—he burst out laughing. A big, hearty, relieved kind of laugh. "Oh," he said, shaking his head. "Then it's not a problem for you. You know how it works. Go for it!" We both cracked up like two kids sharing an inside joke.

The next morning, he made sure to check on me—just in case. Another time, I was attending a trade show in Moscow as a booth and marketing manager, along with my local sales colleagues. The event was packed, and we were doing well—plenty of foot traffic, solid leads, and good energy all around. Then, one of my colleagues dropped an interesting piece of news: an important decision-maker—an advisor of the Ministry of Transport—would be attending the conference. "But don't even dream of him stopping by our booth," he added. "The guy is surrounded by bodyguards and way too important to notice us." Of course, that only made me more curious. " Given the high number of car accidents at dawn, it would be amazing to introduce him to our road safety solutions," he admitted, "but let's be realistic. It's not happening." Challenge accepted. The next day, I arrived at the booth extra early, determined to get a feel for the logistics of this VIP visit. And, just as I was taking it all in, I spotted him. There he was— walking in our direction. I knew it was him because suddenly, the photographers around him kicked into high-stress mode, scrambling for the best shots.

My local sales colleague hadn't arrived yet, so I grabbed my phone and called him. "You better get here now," I said. "Our guy is definitely visiting our booth." He chuckled. "Girl, I think you're dreaming." I smirked. "I'll give you five minutes. You know my Russian is limited to the word "doroga," so either you get here, or you'll miss the show." Dmitri appeared out of nowhere, his face red and baffled. I swear he must have sprinted across the entire hall to make it to the booth in five minutes. I let out a sigh of relief.

"Follow me—we need to catch our man," I told him. Without a word, he obeyed. Like an arrow, I cut through the crowd, heading straight for the most important person in the trade show. No hesitation. I introduced myself, extending my hand for a handshake. Now, in Russia, men don't usually shake hands with women unless she offers first. I knew that. And I used it to my advantage. His reaction was priceless—stunned at first, then clearly amused by my boldness. I didn't waste time on pleasantries. I dove straight in—talking about traffic accident statistics, the urgent need for improved safety measures, and our excitement to introduce him to our solutions portfolio, backed by solid statistical data. He listened intently, nodding as I spoke. Then came the golden moment. "I've never heard of this possibility before," he admitted. Right in front of me, he turned to his secretary and instructed her to find a time slot for us. And just like that, he showed up at our booth the next day.

We were ready. We knew everything—his pain points, the costs they were incurring from low-quality traffic safety products, the solutions we could offer, and most importantly, the number of car accidents we could help reduce. The stage was set. Within an hour, we had set up a field trial to prove our point—something that would have normally taken us years of work to even get close to. We went all in, working night and day to prepare a rock-solid report to back up our position. And guess what? Everything ran smoothly.

That field trial became the event of the year in our department. And I think my colleagues walked away with an important lesson: people often limit themselves, trapping their potential inside hierarchical thinking. But at the end of the day, it's just a choice. And if it's a choice, we can choose differently—we don't have to be held back by limiting beliefs.

Fast forward to another time— I was in the Emirates with our technical and sales teams, meeting with key decision-makers in the field of road safety. The team had already conducted a field trial, and the results were outstanding. Two years of heavy traffic use, and everything held up perfectly. You'd think that would be enough to convince them, right? Nope. The decision-makers still weren't fully on board. Before the meeting, my local sales colleagues pulled me aside with a little heads-up: "You're going to be the only woman in that room. Most Arabian men don't feel comfortable if they think a woman is giving them orders. No offense, but it's better if you just sit at the table, listen, and don't speak." Ouch. That stung a little. But I nodded and played along. For now. There we were, stepping into the building. The first impression? Rough.

No women in sight in that specific building. Some of the men acted like I was invisible, while others were so shocked to see a female figure that they went out of their way to get my attention—some subtle, some not so much. We sat down at the negotiation table, and the discussion dragged on for hours, going in circles with no agreement in sight. I could see our Head of Technical Marketing—an experienced negotiator—growing more and more frustrated with their indecision.

Meanwhile, I was trying my best to sit still, stay quiet, and let the process play out. But patience? Yeah... not exactly my strong suit. At some point, I thought to myself, enough is enough. Without overthinking it, I stood up. Walked right to the front of the room like I owned the place—like I was stepping onto a stage. Then, with as much authority as I could muster, I said: "Gentlemen, may I have your attention, please?" Silence. Absolute silence. You could hear a pin drop. One man, dressed typically, was staring at me, mouth slightly open, as if I had just performed magic. I took a deep breath and got straight to the point.

I recapped our original goals, the agreements we had already made, and exactly where we were stuck. Then, grabbing a pen, I turned to the flipchart and laid out a roadmap—a clear, logical next step with a realistic timeline. The men looked at each other. Nodded. And just like that, we had an agreement. At the end of the meeting, the decision-makers asked me to visit them again. Well, that was unexpected!

Afterward, we headed straight to our trade show booth as planned. But word travels fast in the market—before we knew it, potential customers were showing up, eager to hear the full story firsthand. Some even came just to meet "the lady from the meeting" in person. Who knew I'd turn into a mini-celebrity overnight? Once we were outside, my colleagues—who had sat through the whole thing with me—couldn't stop laughing. They kept joyfully repeating my words, shaking their heads in disbelief. "Thank goodness that went well!" they said.

"You are crazy! My goodness, what kind of show was that?" Honestly, I don't know if I'd ever do it again if given the chance. But get this—the very same decision-makers in that meeting invited me to attend their conference twice in the following years. Go figure! Looking back, I think growing up in a poor neighborhood gave me a different lens to see the world—not through fear, but through reality. I never let titles or status intimidate me. Instead, I learned to adjust my behavior and vocabulary depending on who I was speaking to. But never once did I measure whether the person in front of me was "more" or "less" important than I was. Because, really—who even decides that?

TWO KINDS OF PEOPLE?

The image of that young man lying lifeless on the floor when I was in the fourth grade haunted me for years. But what truly unsettled me wasn't just the sight—it was the way I described him when my teacher asked about it. I didn't call him "a man." I didn't call him "a stranger."

I called him "uncle." He wasn't my uncle. Not by blood, not by any real connection. But in that moment, that label felt right. And maybe, even at that young age, I was already growing tired of the way we judge people—how we slap labels on them, as if life is as simple as "good" or "bad." Does it really matter that he wasn't my uncle? He was someone's uncle. Someone's brother. Someone's father or son. And just like that, in a single violent moment, he was gone. A life, a story, maybe even a handful of dreams—wiped out.

Every second of every day, we judge. We decide who's "good" and who's "bad" based on our beliefs, our culture, our past experiences. We box people in according to how well (or not) they fit into our expectations. And sure, that might feel normal, even necessary. But what if there's another way? What if, instead of making snap judgments, we trained ourselves to keep an open, peaceful mind? What if we stopped being prisoners of our own assumptions? Because the more we cling to this habit of labeling, the more we trap ourselves in a cycle that never really serves us. And honestly? There has to be a better way.

While I'm a guest on this earth, I want to spend my time seeing people as they are—without preconceptions, without judgment. And if I do slip into judging (because, let's be real, it's bound to happen), I want to have the awareness to choose again. To choose peace instead. Imagine that—a life where we don't judge people based on what our eyes insist on showing us. How would that feel? To me, that sounds like true freedom. The kind that comes from choosing peace over the need to be right.

BECOMING A VOLUNTEER IN A JAIL

At least in Germany, being affiliated with a church makes it easier to get accepted as a prison volunteer. It's like having an invisible key—one that unlocks doors most people never get to step through. But that wasn't my case. My path into the prison system started differently. It all began with a visit to a friend who had been volunteering at the same facility for over ten years. As she talked about her experiences, her eyes sparkled, her voice full of passion. She spoke about the women she met—many of them from South America—who had been caught up in the illusion of a "big trip" that turned into a nightmare in the illicit drug trade.

Her stories painted vivid pictures in my mind—women who once had dreams, hopes, and plans for brighter futures, are now reduced to mere numbers in a foreign prison, unable to even understand the language around them. And yet, despite the bleakness of it all, my friend had found something meaningful. She spoke about the power of connection—how a simple visit, a shared moment, and a few words of kindness could bring warmth to a place that felt so cold. I could almost see it. These women, sitting across from her in the visiting room, their eyes flickering with something close to hope—even if just for a fleeting moment. Her passion was contagious. It made me feel the weight of their stories, their struggles pressing into me. I could feel it tugging at something inside me. "It's not just about visiting them," she said. "It's about helping them see a way out of the darkness—even if it's just a glimmer."

Her words lingered in my mind, echoing long after the conversation ended. A part of me felt drawn to it as if something was calling me to step forward. But at the same time? I was skeptical. Me? Leaving my comfort zone to work with women sentenced to prison in Germany? It felt like a stretch—one I wasn't sure I was ready to make. She told me she had just started a master's degree and would need to take a break from her duties.

Long story short—she never came back. And just like that, I found myself stepping into the unexpected role of mentoring women in a German prison. To say I felt out of place would be an understatement. I mean, my background? Chemistry and an MBA. No psychology degree, no formal training in social sciences—nothing that screamed "qualified to work in a prison". I kept asking myself: What am I even doing here? Can I really make a difference?

But then, I had a realization. In my career, I'd tackled complicated problems, managed clashing personalities, and led teams through messy, high-stakes changes. I'd trained myself to think analytically, to break big, overwhelming issues into smaller, solvable pieces. So, I thought, why not apply the same logic here? Maybe mentoring in a prison wasn't so different from the challenges I had already faced—just with a completely new (and slightly intimidating) backdrop. I learned that the best problem-solvers don't always follow a set blueprint. They adapt, connect the dots that others miss, and find solutions in unexpected ways. So, I figured—why not do the same?

I decided to take the skills I already had, like problem-solving and conflict resolution, and use them to make an impact in a completely different setting.

Becoming a volunteer was actually pretty straightforward. First, an in-person interview. Then, apply for a certificate of good conduct. After that, a couple of hours of safety training and a detailed rundown of all the do's and don'ts. That last part? The rules? Yeah, that was the toughest for me. At one point, I caught myself thinking, Why in the world am I putting myself in this risky situation? One slip-up—one forgotten detail—and I'd be in serious trouble. And trust me, "Ms. Justice" isn't exactly known for second chances. The whole scene felt surreal.

Being inside a jail for the first time is unsettling. You look around and feel... out of place. The employees— police officers in crisp uniforms—carry themselves with an air of strict authority. No warmth, no sympathy, just business. Then came the rules. They read them out loud, one by one—stern, unwavering. All the things I could and couldn't do. The legal consequences if I messed up. The penalties. The punishments. It was intimidating, to say the least. I had to focus—watch my breath, stay present, and remind myself why I was there. Be helpful. Stay in the moment. Resist the urge to just get up and walk away. It took effort. A lot of it. But in the end? Totally worth it. I got accepted.

WHY DO YOUNG PEOPLE ENGAGE IN DRUG SMUGGLING?

I couldn't help but ask myself this question when I first started volunteering. Of course, the reasons vary, but after six years in this work, I've noticed some common patterns. From what I've seen, the motivations for smuggling drugs—whether from South America to Europe or, in the case of amphetamines, from Europe to South America—often depend on the country.

Take Colombia, for example. While financial gain is a factor for some, many young people don't have a choice. I've heard heartbreaking stories from detainees who were forced into the trade under the threat that their families would suffer if they refused. And if they got caught? Losing the drugs meant more than just an arrest—it meant serious consequences back home. Each case is different, but these stories have given me a deeper understanding of the hidden realities behind drug smuggling. For smugglers from Brazil, the story plays out a little differently. Their motivation? Usually, financial. These recruits don't just stumble into the job—they're chosen. Handpicked based on their appearance. The ideal candidate? Young, usually white, unobtrusive, and preferably fluent in English. Basically, someone who looks like an innocent tourist or a student on a dream vacation. Sometimes, it's not just solo travelers. Couples get selected. Even families with kids.

The pitch is simple: "It's easy. You get a free trip to Europe, have some fun, and come back rich." The dealers make it sound foolproof, bragging about how they've done it countless times without ever getting caught. Seasoned pros, they say. And for someone drowning in debt, struggling to pay tuition, dreaming of starting a business, or just craving those coveted Gucci bags and luxury brands—well, the offer can feel impossible to refuse. Before they know it, the ticket is booked. Bags are packed. And they're on a plane, about to step into a world they can't escape.

If you grew up in poverty, with parents who never had the chance to chase big dreams—maybe they didn't even finish school—you probably see the world differently than someone who's never known what it's like to go without.

But here's something surprising: when it comes to drug trafficking, the young people targeted for overseas smuggling aren't necessarily those who dropped out of school early or struggled financially. No, the real targets are often the ones who finished high school or are even attending university. The ones who can speak well, carry themselves with confidence and make a good impression. Drug traffickers don't just offer money— they appeal to ego. They tell these young people how special they are, how much potential they have, and how many incredible experiences they're missing out on. And for someone struggling with self-esteem, that kind of attention can be dangerously persuasive. In the rush of the moment, they don't stop to think about the consequences—the heartbreak they might bring to their own family, the damage they're fueling by supporting a criminal industry that destroys lives.

Herbert Spencer, the English sociologist and philosopher, once said: "Every man has the freedom to do as he wills, provided he infringes not on the equal freedom of any other man." A powerful idea—but looking at the world today, we're still far from living up to it.

Girls often get swept up by the charm, the sweet words, the flattering attention—only to realize too late that what seemed like a dream was actually a trap. They think they're stepping into something exciting, but in reality, they're giving up their freedom for captivity.

Over the years, I've met some young women who, in our first conversation, were convinced they had done nothing wrong. To them, society was to blame for their situation. They believed they were closer than ever to success, and watching their dream fall apart felt unbearable.

This, of course, is denial—a coping mechanism, a way to shield themselves from the painful truth. Fortunately, not all of them think this way. And honestly? It's all understandable.

As a volunteer, the best thing you can do at this stage is simple: listen. No judging, no lecturing—just be a source of peace. If you want to bring peace, you must embody it yourself. After all, how can we create peace for others if we don't cultivate it within? And here's the thing—once they realize you're not there to judge, something shifts. They start to reflect, to process, to see their actions in a new light. They begin looking forward instead of dwelling on the past. That's when real change happens.

MY FIRST PRISON MENTORING EXPERIENCE

The day had finally arrived—my first-time volunteering in a prison. I had spent the entire day running through what I would say, how I could offer comfort, and constantly reminding myself: Listen more than you speak. Doubt crept in. Am I even the right person for this? The questions swirled in my mind, making me second-guess myself. But after hours of overthinking, I took a deep breath and reminded myself—I was here to give my best. That was enough. I realized I didn't need a perfect speech or a detailed plan. Inspiration would come. So I asked myself: If I were in prison, thousands of miles from home, in a country where I didn't speak the language, far from my family, friends, and even my pets... what would I want the most?

That question changed everything. Suddenly, it all made sense. My job wasn't to have all the answers—it was to be present. To listen. To show empathy. So that's exactly where I started. Small but powerful steps: listening, offering understanding, and asking the kinds of questions that led to real, meaningful conversations. Arriving at the prison was a whole experience in itself.

First, I had to wait—several long minutes—because a police bus had just pulled up, surrounded by officers. The whole scene felt intense, almost cinematic. For a second, I wondered if I should've turned around and left. At the front desk, I quickly learned that bringing in any personal belongings was a no-go. Everything had to be locked away outside. No phone, no wallet, no distractions. Just me, stepping into an entirely different world. Once inside, I went through an x-ray scan—head to toe. They weren't taking any chances. Finally, I was led to the waiting area, where I sat, nerves buzzing, heart pounding.

A few minutes later, an officer appeared and motioned for me to follow. The meeting room was just ahead. Before leaving me, they pointed out the emergency call button—just in case I needed help or wanted to be escorted out once the meeting was over. I sat down. Took a deep breath. And then, I waited Suddenly, the door swung open. A woman stepped in, followed by a policeman. She was stunning—probably around 20 years old—with long, smooth, shiny hair. There was something confident about the way she carried herself, and her outfit. Impeccable. I blinked, confused. This can't be her. She must be a prison employee, I thought.

In my head, prisoners wore uniforms, just like in the movies. Or at the very least, they looked miserable, broken, maybe even intimidating. Anything but this. But then, she walked right up to me and spoke—in Portuguese. Oh. Oh. "Dear God, she's the prisoner," I realized.

She flashed a warm smile. "*Oi!* I'm Jana," she said, her voice bubbling with excitement. She went on and on about how thrilled she was to finally have a visitor— after two whole years. Of course, prisoners saw their attorneys from time to time, but from the way she spoke, that didn't seem to count.

I gave a quick introduction—how long I had lived in Germany, and how excited I was to finally meet her in person. She, on the other hand, introduced herself in great detail, almost as if she were trying to remember who she was—or maybe just relishing the feeling of being someone again. She was from the North of Brazil and had an older stepsister. As she spoke, her voice warmed with nostalgia, weaving vivid memories of home—the smell of freshly baked bread at the bakery, the rhythm of the waves crashing at the beach, the noise, the traffic, the vibrant flowers. But above all, she missed her motorcycle. Her bike wasn't just transportation—it was her freedom, her identity, her most trusted companion. It had taken her through countless adventures, becoming almost a part of her, like a personal brand. I couldn't help but notice that her hands trembled slightly, but her eyes locked onto mine with an intensity that made me feel like she was trying to read my thoughts. Then, suddenly, she stopped mid-sentence, let out a self-conscious laugh, and shook her head. "Wow, I've been talking like a runaway train," she said, almost embarrassed. I grinned.

To be honest, I was relieved. In my ignorance, I had expected to meet someone completely broken, someone drowning in sadness. Instead, here she was—full of life, full of stories. Before I knew it, our hour was up. We said our goodbyes warmly, promising to meet every two weeks. As I walked away, I thought to myself: "Piece of cake. I can do this."

After that encounter, something strange started happening. I began dreaming of a woman—always dressed in dark clothing, sitting with her head down, looking completely lost, swallowed by sadness. I had no clue who she was or what she wanted. And honestly? I had no idea why I kept dreaming about her in the first place. But something about her stuck with me. So, before bed, I started saying little prayers for her, whoever she was. Then, the dreams shifted. Suddenly, she wasn't just sitting there anymore.

She was behind bars—prison bars. At some point, I started experiencing what felt like lucid dreams—where I was fully aware that I was the one dreaming. And in that strange, in-between state, I began experimenting. I told myself to picture her surrounded by light. At first, it was just an idea. But then, something incredible happened—she reacted. It was as if she could see the light, feel it. That moment filled me with certainty. I knew, deep down, that I was doing exactly what I was meant to do.

Meanwhile, my visits to Jana became more comfortable. The tension that once hovered between us started to fade, and trust quietly settled in its place. Little by little, she let me in, sharing the pieces of herself she had kept hidden. Then, one day, she confided in me. She was addicted to heroin. She was constantly on medication. Hearing those words, I felt the weight of what she carried. But more than anything, I knew what this meant for me—I'd have to navigate her unpredictable mood swings, to understand that some days would be harder than others.

The social workers never shared much about the inmates—just their age. No details about their sentences, how long they'd be inside, any psychological issues, addictions—nothing. I figured it was all due to the German Data Protection Regulation. Instead, I had to learn things the natural way—through conversations, if the inmates chose to open up.

Jana, for example. Because of the medication, she had those classic highs and lows of addiction, and her hands shook quite a bit. But other than that? She had an impressive ability to focus for hours. She was deeply religious too and would sometimes ask me to pray with her. One day, during a visit, she finally told me how she ended up in the dangerous world of drug smuggling.

Her relationship with her parents was full of love, but she never felt truly understood—like she was constantly falling short of their expectations. University didn't excite her, money was always tight, and, little by little, she started slipping. A few months before the trip that would change everything, she moved out of her parents' home and dove headfirst into a life of non-stop parties, sleepless nights, and reckless choices.

Drugs became part of the mix—at first, just marijuana. Then cocaine. And eventually... heroin. Whenever she needed money, she'd come back home like nothing had changed, calm, composed, playing the role perfectly. But it never lasted. Before long, her patience would wear thin. She'd snap over the smallest things, her temper flaring like a matchstick. One minute, she was fine; the next, she was exploding in anger. It didn't take long for her parents to catch on. They saw the shift, the pattern. And eventually, they made a tough decision—they stopped giving her money. That's when desperation kicked in.

With no other way to fund her habit, she started stealing from home, taking whatever, she could sell for quick cash. But even that wasn't enough. That's when the realization hit her—without the drugs, she felt like nothing. A nobody, in her own words. The high became more than just an escape; it was her only escape. Her best friend. The only thing that made the emptiness bearable, even if just for a little while. And soon, getting money for her next fix became all that mattered. She started exchanging sex for cash or drugs—whatever it took to keep the cycle going.

At a party one night, a dealer approached her with an offer too tempting to refuse. At that moment, she thought she had struck gold—the perfect solution to all her problems. With the money, she could finally start a small business, prove herself, and surprise her family in the best way possible. As for "the drug thing"? She was convinced she had it under control. She could stop anytime she wanted. But reality had other plans. A prison sentence in Germany? That was never part of her script.

Months behind bars forced her to confront a painful truth. Shame and regret clung to her like a second skin. When she finally gathered the courage to call her parents, the weight of her choices hit harder than ever. For the first time, she truly understood—they had always loved her, just in their own way. They had only wanted the best for her. But by then, it was too late. No one could fix this but her. Life in prison turned out to be far less daunting than she had feared. She found solace in education, quickly picking up German, which gave her both a sense of purpose and a way to connect with others.

To support herself, she took a job in the prison, earning money for essentials like phone calls, stamps, clothing, and personal care items. The work gave her a sense of belonging, and she excelled at it. But it was her creativity that truly set her apart. She had a natural talent for fashion design, something she hadn't fully explored before. With whatever materials she could find—worn-out blankets, old sheets—she began crafting jackets, pullovers, pants, skirts, and even unique accessories like scarves and hats. She played with bold, unexpected color combinations, once designing a pair of pants with a patchwork of orange and teal that seemed to pulse with energy. As her skills grew, so did her ambition.

She started dreaming of something bigger—of one day becoming a famous designer and showcasing her creations to the world. It was ironic, really; her mother had tried to teach her to sew years ago, but only within the prison walls did she truly embrace it, as if the craft had been waiting for the right moment to emerge. I would have loved to order a suit made by her own hands—something with an edgy twist and a touch of her signature style. But prison rules were strict. No special treatment, no exceptions.

Her sharp intelligence quickly earned her a top position in the prison laundry, where she thrived at organizing tasks and streamlining the workflow. Her keen eye for detail and efficiency made her an invaluable asset. But success came at a cost. Jealousy brewed among the other inmates, who saw her rise as a threat to their own standing. The hostility began subtly—snide remarks, cold stares—but soon escalated into outright sabotage. Though she did her best to stay composed, not every provocation went unanswered. Still, she reminded herself that dignity mattered more than retaliation. Yet, the tension lingered, each challenge testing her patience, resilience, and the strength of her resolve. Then came a moment when she almost acted on impulse—ready to strike back at a provocation that, had she followed through, would have cost her months, perhaps even years, of her dream of freedom. I knew I had to step in before she made a choice she'd regret.

I approached her with a piece of Buddhist wisdom: "Never let anger take hold, for in one day you might burn all the wood you've gathered, the very wood that could have kept you warm for a year." The wisdom hit deep, and in that instant, she knew it was time to let go of the urge and choose a different path.

The dreams with the mysterious woman continued. Each time, she seemed more aware of my presence, as if she knew I was somehow part of her world. At first, her eyes would search the space around her, curious but uncertain. Then, over time, her expression softened, and she began to look happier. It was as if she had come to expect me there as if my presence brought her comfort.

One afternoon, I went to visit Jana as usual. I sat in the small meeting room, waiting as the familiar buzz of prison life hummed around me. When she finally entered, something was different. Her shoulders slumped, her steps slower than usual. She hugged me— longer than ever before as if she had been waiting for this moment for ages. Her grip was firm, almost desperate. I hesitated, unsure of what to say.

When we sat down, she took a deep breath and asked, "Do you remember when I told you I had a sister?" I nodded. "Yes. But you haven't mentioned her since." She lowered her gaze, tracing a crack on the table with her fingertip. Then, in a quiet voice, she said, "She's in prison too. In Spain." I blinked. "What?". "She was arrested a month before me," she continued her voice barely above a whisper. "I didn't know until recently."

A heavy silence settled between us. The weight of her words hung in the air, shifting everything I thought I knew about her story. She told me she'd received a letter from her a few weeks ago. In it, she described feeling completely hopeless—she had no appetite and couldn't find the energy to get out of bed. Her words were full of regret, especially about what had happened to Jana. Her stepsister felt guilty, convinced that if only she had reached out sooner to tell her she'd been caught, she wouldn't have made the trip. Her voice cracked as she spoke, and I could sense how devastated she was. She feared the worst and even wondered if she might harm herself.

My heart ached as I listened. What struck me most, though, was how familiar her story felt—this woman, with her pain and regret, was the same one I had seen in my dreams. I didn't mention the dreams, but I reassured her that she was getting better. I encouraged her to send her mental messages every day—remind her that it wasn't her fault, that she loved her, and that together, they'd come through this stronger than before.

Four weeks later, she received another letter from her imprisoned stepsister. This time, her tone was entirely different. She was feeling stronger and had started making plans for the future. She couldn't believe they were both living through such a nightmare, but she was confident that a brighter future awaited them both, and that a new chapter was about to begin. After that letter, the dreams of the mysterious woman stopped—just like that. They never returned. I believe our encounter, in some way, was fulfilled.

In prison, Jana faced not only the harshness of her environment but also the battle within herself. Women who spend years incarcerated often long for a romantic connection—someone who sees them, listens to them, or simply shows they care. It can almost feel like an escape from the grim reality of confinement. In such circumstances, many women turn to love stories with fellow inmates, seeking solace in a bond that provides a fleeting sense of warmth and human connection. Jana wasn't immune to this.

When a new woman arrived on her block, Jana felt an undeniable pull toward her. What began as a brief, intense connection quickly flared into a passionate, fiery affair—wild and all-consuming, like a volcano suddenly erupting. The heat was overwhelming and intense, and yet, just as quickly as it had ignited, it began to cool and fade. When it was over, they parted ways as though nothing had ever happened—leaving behind nothing but a memory of a love story that was never meant to last.

I often wonder how Sigmund Freud would interpret such situations. He once said, "How bold one gets when one is sure of being loved." Would he view these fleeting, intense relationships as a reflection of unmet emotional needs or as a coping mechanism for the emotional and physical isolation of prison life? From Freud's perspective, these relationships might be seen as driven by a deep desire for emotional connection, affection, and validation—fundamental human needs often intensified in the isolating environment of prison. He might have said it allows the individuals to avoid deeper vulnerability or attachment, thus protecting themselves from the potential heartbreak of abandonment or loss—emotions that likely knew well. Maybe, Freud might interpret these relationships as a manifestation of repressed desires—sexual, affectionate, or otherwise—that would typically find healthier outlets in the outside world like eating chocolate or buying a luxurious bags. In the extreme restrictions of prison, the usual avenues for affection are confined, and the short-lived nature of these bonds could be seen as an unconscious attempt to be noticed, cared for, missed by someone. "He might have argued that physical intimacy could act as a temporary escape from the emotional pain of imprisonment—a brief way to feel alive and desired in a place where one might otherwise feel invisible or powerless." But, of course, this is something better left to the psychoanalysts among us.

THE GIRL THAT WAS NOT FROM COPACABANA

I had been invited by the prison where I volunteered to accompany a new inmate. As usual, no details about her situation were provided. Waiting in that room, not knowing who would show up at the door or what they would be like, always felt strange. Dalva wasn't from Copacabana; she came from a nearby *comunidade*—the term used for slums in Brazil.

She entered the room hurriedly, a blonde woman with long hair, slightly underweight, and short in stature, dressed in casual sportswear. She rushed in as if she had no time to waste. She introduced herself briefly before launching into the details of her situation. Dalva explained that she, her husband, and their 5-year-old child had been arrested right after stepping off the plane in Frankfurt. She shared how badly she had been treated in jail, how her child had been sent back to Brazil, and how her husband was also incarcerated.

All of this, she insisted, should never have happened. They should have let her go immediately. Wow... I waited for her to pause, catching her breath before I briefly introduced myself. It was clear she was caught in a whirlwind of thoughts, struggling to find her words. I let her speak as much as she needed until our time was up. The next time we met, Dalva seemed calmer, her emotions more under control. She began to open up, revealing the tangled web of events that had led her here. She told me how her family had been involved with drug dealers in Rio de Janeiro's *"morro"*—the hills where the city's slums are found. Her voice softened as she explained the burden that weighed heavily on her heart: her mother was seriously ill and bedridden, and her second son back home, who had mental disabilities, needed constant care.

She had left him with a family friend while she made the dangerous smuggling trip with her husband. The five members of her family lived in a single house in the slums, struggling with extreme poverty and the lack of privacy. Her mother and son needed medications and treatments that the public health system could not provide. When they were arrested at the airport, Dalva's world seemed to shatter. Her son was taken into custody, and without his parents, was sent back to Brazil.

Dalva was convinced that she had done nothing "so bad" and felt that the German justice system had been unnecessarily harsh. With her mother in critical condition and her son's needs pressing, she held onto the hope that the courts might show mercy and release her sooner. One day, Dalva seemed more relaxed, and more open to conversation.

We began discussing our futures—what we were good at, what we dreamed of. It turned out that she had a deep love for baking. The prison kitchen staff adored her cakes and pastries, a small but bright spot in her otherwise grim reality. I picked up on this and encouraged her to explore it further. I suggested that she imagine herself back in her community, opening a café, filled with delightful cakes and pastries—perhaps even including some traditional German cakes she had learned to appreciate. As she listened, I encouraged her to consider sharing her journey with others. Her story of spending three years in a German prison, and the lessons she had learned, could inspire those around her. She could talk about the challenges—learning a new language, adjusting to different food, or even the simple yet significant challenge of dealing with hard water that made our hair frizzy, as if we had stuck our fingers in a 220-volt socket.

There was potential for her to be a speaker at local schools, and universities, or even start a social media platform like Instagram to reach others. She could show how her experience had transformed her, helping to motivate young people to make better choices. Her eyes sparkled with a glimmer of hope, like two diamonds caught in the light.

She seemed to enjoy these thoughts of possibility, a rare moment of joy amidst the bleakness. But, as with every conversation, she would inevitably circle back to the unfairness of it all. She often started by lamenting her son's and mother's condition, both so desperately in need of her care. No one seemed to care about them as much as she did. And each time, I reminded her that the situation was beyond her control now. Her son was safe, her mother was receiving attention, and all she could do was wait for the legal decisions to unfold. It was difficult at times, sitting with her in such a state of frustration, feeling helpless.

All I could offer was a listening ear and a new perspective. But in those moments, I wondered if even that small act of encouragement was enough to spark the change she so desperately needed. A few times, after we said our goodbyes, I would sit in my car for a moment, feeling overwhelmed. In those moments, frustration would well up inside me, and I'd cry out for help or wonder how Dalva couldn't manage her anxiety.

But then it hit me—what I was really seeing was my own weakness in her. I realized how many times I had spent days, even weeks, consumed by anxious thoughts, waiting desperately for immediate results. Psychologists say that we often project onto others what we dislike about ourselves. Suddenly, I understood. I thought back to the times I had applied for a job and couldn't stand the wait for that confirmation email or phone call. Or when I desperately wanted to get pregnant with my second child and expected it to happen right away, only to face months of waiting. Those 14 days of waiting to take a pregnancy test, hoping for a positive result, drove me to the brink every single time.

Then, I reminded myself: that I was not in a position to judge anyone. Becoming impatient would only undermine my goal of being truly helpful to Dalva. I remembered one of my favorite stories about Mahatma Gandhi, which helped me shift my perspective. A woman and her young son had visited Gandhi at his ashram. The mother explained, "My son can't stop eating sugar. Please tell him to stop." Gandhi listened patiently and then asked the woman to return in two weeks. When they came back, Gandhi looked at the boy and simply said, "Stop eating sugar." The mother, confused, asked, "Why didn't you tell him this two weeks ago?" Gandhi smiled and replied, "Madam, two weeks ago, I was still eating sugar."

There I was, perfectly imperfect, trying to fix the world I had created. I rolled up my sleeves, determined to do better. I was ready to be more prepared for the next encounter, resisting the urge to get swept up in negative thoughts that I felt powerless to change. I dove into researching free entrepreneurial courses in Portuguese, imagining a business canvas in my mind—an idea I couldn't wait to discuss the next time we met.

When she began her familiar rhetoric about the unfairness of the world and the people in it, I patiently listened, waiting for the right moment to shift the conversation. Once I had her attention again, I steered it toward our dream café idea in Rio de Janeiro, eager to take it to the next level. I simplified complex business concepts like strategy, market intelligence, and differentiation—using examples that made them easy to grasp. I wanted her to understand how we could stand out from the crowd without feeling overwhelmed. To my surprise, she was both amazed and excited, embracing ideas that were new to her but seemed to click deep down.

In her own words, Dalva began spinning the idea further. She suggested visiting neighboring cafés to learn how they operated. She planned to save part of her prison wages to invest in kitchen equipment and start offering cakes and pastries to local bakeries. The goal was to build enough capital to eventually rent a small spot in a tourist area. She even dreamed of launching a website to offer her products on demand. We even brainstormed potential names for the café: "In God We Trust" or "Cake Your Way."

She loved the idea. Dalva began to dream of opening her own café, providing jobs for her family, and becoming a successful businesswoman. We spent hours refining these ideas, even after that first conversation. But despite her excitement, she still struggled to accept her fate, holding onto the hope that she would soon be released due to family circumstances.

Unfortunately, our inspiring exchange about launching a café was short-lived. One day, Dalva asked me something that caught me completely off guard. "Can you help me get out of here?" It was the most uncomfortable moment of my time volunteering—and the only time an inmate had ever made such a request. I explained, as gently as I could, that I was a volunteer there to make her time in prison more bearable. I had no training, no qualifications, and no authority to do anything beyond that. She was deeply disappointed with my answer, and after that, she started making excuses to avoid meeting with me—headaches, stomachaches, anything to stay away.

After discussing the situation with my official contact at the prison, we concluded that Dalva no longer wanted my support. This marked the shortest of my volunteer experiences, lasting just five months. I sincerely hope that, despite how it ended, she was able to take something positive from our time together.

THE FAITHFUL INTERIOR DESIGNER

Once again, it was time to sit in the waiting room and wait for my new encounter. When she entered, I couldn't help but notice how small she was in stature. At first glance, you might have thought she lacked presence, but there was an undeniable glow about her that drew your attention. This young woman, Laura, was from the Northwest of Brazil. She had lost a brother in a car crash some years before she was imprisoned. She had studied interior design and, back home, worked alongside her husband in their business—designing and crafting custom furniture for all budgets. Things had been going well until a major financial crisis struck.

As their expenses grew, they found themselves sinking deeper into debt. They sold their cars to pay off some bills, but soon they couldn't even afford their rent.

The strain took a heavy toll on their relationship, and they saw no way out. That's when Laura heard about the "dream trip," a chance for a fresh start. Desperate, she decided to try it herself.

Sad shifts in people's lives happen all the time. Without a clear sense of direction, the mind can feel like an empty canvas, waiting to be filled by external influences. It's like drifting aimlessly—no solid ground beneath you, just going wherever the current takes you. "If it worked for them, it should work for me." That hope gives them confidence, solidifying decisions they've already made. And then, the dream crumbles. She convinced her husband that this trip would change everything. They'd earn enough to settle their debts, and this desperate measure would never be necessary again. Together, they made the choice, clinging to the hope that things would turn out okay. She reached out to the dealers, and her ability to inspire trust worked in her favor—she was quickly pulled into the operation.

Days later, she was on her way. But when she arrived at her destination, the routine check didn't go as planned. Her nerves betrayed her, and soon, tears flowed as the reality of the situation set in. From there, it was clear she had something to hide. It didn't take long for the authorities to discover the well-hidden and cleverly disguised cocaine. The first few hours were a nightmare—endless questioning in an unfamiliar world, with no way to escape.

Eight months had passed, and now, here we were together for the first time. During one of our encounters, she broke down. The phone calls with her loved ones were gut-wrenching, especially the voice of her little daughter, asking when she'd be coming home. That single question nearly shattered her. Her husband, however, seemed to be pulling away. During family calls, his absence was palpable—he didn't respond to her letters. To make matters worse, he sent their daughter to live with her parents and began attending parties. The last thing she heard was that he had started an affair.

I tried to understand what drove her—her hobbies, passions and hopes. One thing that stood out was her deep faith in Jesus and Mary, and it soon became the center of our connection. For weeks, our conversations revolved around prayer, and sharing personal experiences of the Divine. One day, she shared a dream with me—Mother Mary had visited her in prison. The joy and excitement in her voice were contagious, filling the room with an energy I hadn't expected. Each time I left her, she would ask me to pray for her, always grateful, always patient, and never complained about the other inmates.

Unfortunately, I wasn't allowed to bring in magazines or books, so we had to get creative when discussing the latest trends in interior design. We drew pictures in the air, communicating with our hands and feet. I'm not particularly artistic myself, but I was amazed by how she described the possibilities—glass, steel, calming greens, soothing greys, and earth tones that could transform a space into a sanctuary for both mental well-being and beauty. She spoke with such passion about how these effects were backed by scientific research, her enthusiasm adding a new layer to our conversations.

Her favorite topic was the concept of "open space." She described it as the art of designing rooms that foster connection—using elevated platforms, low-rise partitions, and contrasting flooring to create a "virtual" separation between spaces, all while keeping things visually open and inclusive. I couldn't help but think, wow, this is way more interesting than studying chemistry!

One day, when I arrived, she seemed particularly down. She was deeply concerned about another inmate with whom she had formed a close bond. The woman's husband had just been sentenced to seven years in prison, and she was struggling to cope. "My friend won't eat, and she's so depressed. I don't know how to help her," she said. "I relate to her situation so much, I can't see a way out either. I feel completely powerless... totally depressed."

In that moment, I thought about how easy it is to feel at peace when life is going well—when you've got your job, family, and friends in place. But as soon as challenges arise, everything shifts. We lose that sense of peace, and in that loss, we often forget how to give it to others. You can only give what you have, after all. To give, we must first receive, and we must have it within ourselves. Then, an inspiration struck. I remembered an ecumenical mass I had attended at my company, where the priest had read a passage from the Old Testament about King Elijah.

To summarize in my own words: this king believed he could change the world through sheer force. But when that didn't work, he retreated to the top of a mountain to commune with God. During his time there, an earthquake shattered the ground, but God was not in the earthquake. A fire raged, but God was not in the fire. A strong wind howled, but God was not in the wind. Then, suddenly, a calm and gentle whisper arose—and that's when he heard God's voice. In other words, everything comes down to the mind—both our tribulations and our peace.

It's all about perception... essentially, a choice we make. The choice to be at peace. The choice to give peace. Somehow, this message struck a deep chord with her. She became emotional, thanking me for the reminder. I truly admired her faith and trust that everything would eventually work out. But one day, while talking to her parents back in Brazil, she sensed something was wrong. It was like they were hiding something from her.

She insisted they tell her what was going on, convinced that something wasn't right. I suppose moms just have that kind of intuition. After a moment of hesitation, her parents opened up. They told her that her four-year-old daughter had decided to climb to the top of a playground structure, despite the rain. Unfortunately, she slipped and fell, hitting her head. She was rushed to the hospital for observation, but thankfully, she had been released and was doing fine. The news shattered her. The thought that she wasn't there to protect her daughter, to hold her, to make it better—it was too much. Her parents reassured her that her little girl was fine, hungry, and full of energy, as curious as ever. Still, a deep ache lingered. She couldn't help but ask if her estranged husband had been informed. Her parents explained they had tried to reach him but with no success. She was stunned by how much he had changed—especially at a time when love, support, and respect were needed most.

On another visit, she was inconsolable. This would be the first birthday of her daughter that she would miss, all because of the poor decisions she had made. Her parents—loving and devoted, as always—had organized a small party to celebrate their granddaughter. Despite being in their 70s, they found new strength and purpose in caring for her. They invited neighborhood children to the party, and although the situation was far from ideal, they did everything they could to make her life feel as normal as possible.

Their unwavering commitment to raising their granddaughter with love and care gave them the energy to navigate this unexpected chapter in their lives. It's hard to imagine what people are capable of when they're in financial distress and see no way out. A year had passed since Laura's husband had left their 4-year-old daughter with her maternal grandparents. Then, out of the blue, he showed up at their house, demanding to take his daughter back. At first, Laura's mother held a glimmer of hope—maybe he wasn't as bad as they had thought, or perhaps he had regretted his actions. But that hope was quickly shattered.

He wasn't there out of remorse; he gave them an ultimatum: either return his daughter or pay him compensation for keeping her from him. Her father had to remind him that he was the one who had abandoned their daughter in the first place. He told him to be thankful she was healthy, happy, and well-cared for. According to Laura, he didn't ask about his daughter's well-being, and didn't care if she needed anything—it was all about him and his demands. Her parents, feeling powerless and shaken, kindly asked him to leave their home—but even as he left, they were left standing on shaky ground. His presence had felt like a storm cloud, hovering above them, threatening to break at any moment. Would he hire a lawyer? Would they lose a legal battle? Their minds raced, uncertain of where the storm would lead.

The situation escalated with each encounter, like waves crashing relentlessly against the shore. At first, he made demands, trying to pressure Laura's parents with threats of legal action. His presence grew darker, a shadow that loomed over them, like a storm on the horizon. Though initially firm in their refusal, Laura's parents began to feel the weight of uncertainty growing heavier by the day. The thought of a legal battle haunted them. They imagined courtrooms, lawyers, and the terrifying possibility of losing their granddaughter before their daughter would ever be released from prison. The fear dug deeper into their hearts. Their son-in-law seemed only interested in parties and women. How could he possibly raise their granddaughter?

Then, one day, a call came from someone claiming to be a lawyer. He said he had prepared a series of legal documents demanding a formal agreement that would allow his client—Laura's husband—to take custody of their granddaughter. Already exhausted by his relentless pursuit, Laura's parents felt cornered. The pressure was suffocating, an invisible vice tightening around them. Laura's father, usually calm and composed, was pushed to his limits. He met with the lawyer, trying to make sense of the legal complexities. But with each new detail, the ground seemed to shift beneath him. He began to question whether they could really protect their granddaughter. The fear of losing her gnawed at him, an ache that wouldn't fade, a constant reminder of what was at stake.

Meanwhile, Laura's mother took matters into her own hands. She called social services, desperate for advice. On the phone with the counselor, she poured out her heart, explaining the situation and the overwhelming fear she felt. The counselor, though understanding, could offer little reassurance. "You've been her caregivers for a year," she said. "But the law is unpredictable." It wasn't the comfort Laura's mother had hoped for, but it gave her the resolve to keep pushing forward.

Then came a turning point. After a particularly heated argument, Laura's father spoke with an intensity that cut through the tension in the room. "You don't even know your own daughter. We've raised her, and we know what's best for her." His words were sharp, carrying the weight of months of worry. The lawyer, sensing their unwavering determination, hesitated before quietly advising his client to reconsider his position. Realizing he wasn't going to win without a fight, Laura's husband began to understand that the court proceedings would be long and costly. His demands, once sharp and cutting, started to lose their potency as the emotional toll of the battle became overwhelming. The more he pushed, the clearer it became: the cost was far greater than he had anticipated. Over time, his persistence faded.

Perhaps it was the mounting expenses of the legal battle, or maybe it was the realization that his once powerful threats were now echoing hollow in his mind. Eventually, he gave up, leaving the family in peace.

Exhausted from the fight and disillusioned by the outcome, the storm passed for the moment.

But perhaps there was another reason for his surrender. Laura, in her quiet strength, relentlessly prayed for peace. Together, we would visualize light filling her parents' home, surrounding her husband with peace and forgiveness. Laura managed not to hate him but instead found compassion for his weaknesses. This ritual, which gave her peace and certainty of eventual victory, seemed to work for both of them.

Our Laura was a silent fighter—guided by a blend of visible and invisible helpers, she walked through the storm toward calmer waters. Despite the heartache and uncertainty, she faced, the days passed, and she grew stronger. The constant weight of not being there for her daughter lingered, but it also became a source of motivation.

Slowly, she began to understand that while the past was unchangeable, her future was still in her hands, and the present was hers to shape. She spent more time reflecting on her decisions, understanding that her actions had consequences—not just for herself, but for everyone she loved. Yet, through it all, she learned that we are not defined by our mistakes. What truly matters is how we rise from them.

Her relationship with her parents deepened as they supported her from afar. They provided her with a strength she had sometimes taken for granted, reminding her that family could be a foundation that withstood even the most challenging times.

One day, while speaking with another inmate, Laura had a profound realization: despite everything—despite being separated from her daughter, despite the uncertainty of her future—there was still hope. She began writing letters to her daughter, sharing stories of her own childhood, the lessons she had learned, and the dreams she still held for their future. Even though she couldn't be there physically, she knew she could still be a guiding force in her daughter's life.

The greatest lesson she learned was that life is unpredictable. It can change in an instant. But no matter how far we fall, or how lost we may feel, there is always room for growth, redemption, and for love. She began sharing this lesson with others, using her own experience to inspire those around her. She became a living example of perseverance, showing that even in the darkest circumstances, there is always a way forward. She made a promise to herself that when she was free again, she would give her daughter a future built on love, wisdom, and resilience—the very things she had gained through her own struggles. And when the day finally came that she was released, she walked out of prison a different woman—stronger, wiser, and more determined to make the most of every moment.

Her story became one of redemption, a testament to the fact that no matter how difficult life may get, we always have the power to change, learn, and build a future filled with hope. She had come to realize that the real prison was not the walls that confined her, but the limitations she had once placed on herself. And now, free from those self-imposed barriers, she was ready to live a life of purpose and possibility.

THE UNIVERSITY STUDENT

Leda was a bright 22-year-old university student, studying History, but her heart was no longer in her studies. With dark hair and a voice that could fill a room, she was known for her quick wit and sharp tongue.

Yet, in the midst of her academic pursuit, she became increasingly disillusioned with her future. She started to question if a degree would even be enough to secure a stable life. The temptation of quick wealth, the allure of something more exciting, pulled her away from the books.

Her brother, always protective, tried to talk her out of it. He'd pick her up from the university, call her twice a day, and do whatever he could to keep her on track. He loved her, but he didn't understand why she couldn't see what he did: the risks, the dangers. She promised him she wouldn't go. But deep down, she'd already made up her mind, and her flight tickets were booked. Fearful of what might happen if she stayed, she took the plunge anyway. When she was arrested, the first person she called was him.

Devastation filled their voices as they spoke. "Please wake me up from this nightmare," she kept saying, unable to comprehend what was happening to her life. Despite the chaos, Leda had an incredible mind. Her conversations were deep and thoughtful, often touching on her love for Philosophy and Politics. Her grammar was impeccable, and her sentences carried the weight of an old soul, each word carefully chosen. As we spoke, I saw beyond the surface—a woman caught in a whirlwind of emotions, seeking purpose, perhaps through the very thing that had led her astray. I hoped our discussions would bring her some comfort, even if just for a moment.

In the confines of prison, some women turn inward, exploring their own thoughts and beliefs in ways they hadn't before. For those with even a hint of education or previous exposure to new ideas, the harsh realities of prison life become fertile ground for deep philosophical questioning. They're forced to confront basic questions of morality, justice, equality, and the very meaning of existence. Leda was one such woman.

One day, during their shared work in the kitchen, she was provoked by another inmate. Her emotions surged, and she found herself caught in a spiral of anger. The words exploded from her, desperate and uncontained— each one an outlet for the frustration that had been building inside her. "I hate everyone involved!" she shouted, her voice sharp with fury.

I asked her to explain what had happened. But instead of offering an explanation, Leda's voice raced to justify her actions, defending herself in an almost frantic rhythm. She detailed the others' wrongs, as though constructing a fortress around herself with every word. It was clear she was protecting herself from more than just the incident; the words tumbled out like a shield against the hurt, the judgment, the reality she didn't want to face. Each explanation seemed to trap her deeper in her own defense, as if convincing herself was the only way to survive.

It became clear that Leda was trapped in her own narrative, fixated on the wrongs done to her, unable—or perhaps unwilling—to see beyond her own perspective. Her anger had built a wall around her, brick by brick and it was hard to imagine anything breaking through. I gently interrupted, hoping to offer a shift. "But what would happen if you tried to see things from the other person's point of view?" She paused, the suggestion hanging in the air. For a moment, she simply stared at me, as though the idea itself was something foreign—an unfamiliar language or a mirror that distorted everything she knew.

The silence between us thickened. Shifting her focus from self-defense to introspection wasn't going to be easy, but it felt like the first step toward breaking the cycle of anger that had held her captive for so long. I caught myself wondering: How many times have I thought like this? It's so much easier to stay cool when you're not the one being hurt.

As we sat there, the silence settled into a contemplative stillness. I could see the wheels turning in her mind, though they moved slowly at first—like a train unsure if it should leave the station, hesitant to break free from the weight of old habits. In such situations, it is like being lost in a thick maze, unsure of how to find our way out. In that moment of confusion, if we could just pause and quiet our minds, we might open ourselves to a spark of inspiration. It could come in the form of a phone call, a flash of insight, or even a simple sign—something that guides us toward the solution we've been searching for. In that stillness, we might hear the voice of a friend, or perhaps even a guardian angel, hovering above us, seeing the clear path to freedom. Or maybe we'll hear a gentle whisper: "Be still and listen, my child. Be inspired. Let go of the pain and choose peace instead."

I suggested we try an exercise together. 'Do you remember the Socratic method of questioning? It's a powerful tool to resolve conflicts by asking open-ended questions that spark self-reflection. I know you might not be familiar with it, but at work, I use a technique called the '5 Whys' that helps to get to the root of any issue. Would you like to try it with me?' She was always up for a challenge. "Of course!", she said. I smiled and continued, "I'm going to ask "Why" repeatedly, and you need to answer as clearly as possible. Keep your answers short—just one sentence, or around 30 seconds. Are you ready? There we were.

Leda started: "A girl in the kitchen hates me."

Me: "Why?"

Leda: "She doesn't accept that I'm her supervisor."

Me: "Why?"

Leda: "She thinks she's better qualified."

Me: "Why?"

Leda: "She doesn't like the way I solve problems."

Me: "Why?"

Leda: "I guess she doesn't feel involved in finding solutions."

Me: "Why?"

Leda: "Because I don't ask for anyone's opinion."

Me: "Why?"

Leda: "As a supervisor, I feel like I need to have all the answers."

Me: "Why?" She shifted uncomfortably in her chair, her voice quieter now. "I guess I feel insecure in my position." We paused for a moment. I could tell she was grappling with the weight of her words. She chuckled softly, almost embarrassed.

"Wait, I thought it was supposed to be 5 Whys." I smiled. "It's not about the number; it's about digging deeper until we find the root cause of the problem." Leda took a breath, her expression softening. "It's like everything suddenly clicked—like the pieces of a puzzle I didn't even know I was trying to solve." Her voice dropped to a quieter, more vulnerable tone.

"Deep down, I wanted to fake my answers just to keep my right to be right. But I realized, I'd just be lying to myself." I nodded, feeling the shift in the conversation. "So, it sounds like you're feeling a bit isolated in your role like you're carrying all the responsibility by yourself. How does that make you feel?" Leda exhaled slowly, her shoulders slumping a little. "Yes, that's exactly it. It's overwhelming sometimes. I feel like if I don't have all the answers, people will think I'm weak or incapable." I leaned forward, gently probing, "Do you think asking for help or input from others might show weakness, not strength?" Leda: "I've never really thought about it that way. I guess I always thought supervisors had to have everything under control." Me: "It's understandable. We often think leadership is about having all the answers. But maybe true leadership isn't about being in control—it's about guiding people, encouraging them to find their own answers, and providing input. That's what builds strong, resilient teams. What do you think would happen if you started asking for feedback, or involving others in problem-solving?"

She paused, looking thoughtful. "Maybe it would ease the tension. Maybe the girl would feel more valued, and I'd feel less burdened. But I'm not sure if I'm ready to make that change." Me: "It's okay to feel uncertain. Change takes time. But remember, asking for help doesn't mean you're less capable—it actually makes you a stronger leader. It shows you trust your team and are open to learning and growing together. That builds respect and trust."

Leda said, "You're right. Maybe I can start small—ask for input on smaller tasks first, just to see how it feels." Me: "That sounds like a great plan. And remember, leadership isn't just about guiding—it's about creating an environment where everyone feels heard and valued. When you give people the chance to contribute, you might be surprised at the support you receive. Honestly, I need to practice that too." We both laughed.

SEX IN OUR MINDS, LOVE IN OUR HEARTS

"Life is like riding a bicycle. To keep your balance, you must keep moving," said Albert Einstein. And so, there I was, stepping into a new chapter. Cristina had a presence you couldn't ignore—the kind of person who owned every room she walked into. And she knew it. She knew exactly how to wield that power, to charm, to captivate.

But there was one catch—Cristina fell in love fast. It didn't matter if it was a man or a woman. In her mind, her beauty was irresistible, and she built her entire world around that belief. She'd get a serious stammer anytime she felt anxious about people watching her.

Her family life back in Minas Gerais was anything but stable. Her father had been married three times, and her mother had left when she was young to travel the world with another man. She had siblings and a big family, but her uncle was the one she idolized. To her, he was the most respected figure she had ever known. He had taught her everything—how to fix a car engine, how to build a house.

Then came the man—the one with whispered rumors of drug-related crimes swirling around him. That only added to the thrill. Their relationship was chaotic, a never-ending loop of breakups, reconciliations, and fleeting party encounters. He was a salesman, constantly traveling, never fully present. But Cristina didn't mind. She was a rising social media influencer with thousands of followers and a talented singer, but convinced she had him wrapped around her finger.

She'd say it to me all the time, gesturing dramatically, hands in the air, as if to prove her control over him. As time went on, he invited her to travel with him to Rio de J. The timing was uncanny—just before his invitation, she had a strange, unsettling dream. She was trapped in an unfamiliar place, incarcerated. A voice, distant yet clear, told her she could change her fate—but only if she listened. These kinds of revelations weren't new to her.

She had always trusted her instincts, convinced she knew how to protect herself. So, she shrugged it off. Everything would be just fine. He bought the tickets, and off they went. The trip felt surreal, like something out of a movie. He was effortlessly charming, endlessly romantic, and money? Not a problem. He carried himself like a seasoned traveler, navigating Rio with ease. She was mesmerized, floating in a dream where she was the star. But dreams have a way of turning into nightmares. Within the first three days, things started to feel... off. He would vanish for hours, leaving her alone in the hotel. When he returned, he always had a smooth, convincing story.

Work, errands, unexpected meetings—each explanation wrapped in just enough detail to sound real. Still, something inside her stirred. A whisper of doubt. One day, she called her uncle to share what was happening. Her uncle, clearly alarmed, urged her to come home immediately.

This wasn't a dream anymore—it was turning into a full-blown nightmare. But how could she just walk away? They were about to travel to Europe together! And then, the next surprise. Just before their flight to Germany, he called. There was an "emergency," he said, and she should go ahead with their luggage. He'd meet her there. I know what you're thinking—this sounds like something straight out of a Hollywood thriller. But I promise you, it wasn't.

His luggage had cocaine. She had no idea. She was arrested at the airport. He disappeared, hiding in France—at least until INTERPOL caught up with him much later, according to what she heard.

When I first met her, I expected to see someone broken, but instead, I saw resilience. She had adjusted to her new reality with remarkable strength. She had a natural leadership quality, and before long, she was respected inside the prison. But prison is a game of highs and lows.

One week, she'd be strong and confident. The next, she'd feel like nothing at all. I remember one time, she sat quietly, withdrawn, her gaze fixed on the floor as if the weight of her past was crushing her. "I can't see a way forward," she admitted. "Everything I've done has led me here." I listened, then said, "What if this isn't the end of your story, but a new chapter? What if your mistakes are just lessons in disguise?"

At that moment, I saw a spark in her eyes—a flicker of possibility she hadn't allowed herself to consider before. For me, it wasn't about fixing everything all at once. It was about planting seeds of change, one conversation at a time.

"My dearest friend, whatever you say isn't going to change anything. But... thank you anyway.", she told me. Wow. That was honest. "Just think about it," I added. "If you're here anyway, why not make the best of it? You know the saying—' When life gives you lemons, make lemonade." She didn't reply right away, but something had shifted. And soon enough, she started planning a new beginning. It wouldn't be easy—there would be bumps and twists along the way. But hey, that's life.

Then, life threw another curveball. Cristina developed a persistent migraine shortly after slightly twisting her ankle during a sports class. She was concerned that it could be something more serious, such as a brain tumor, given its presence in her family history. The prison had medical staff on-site, but her condition required the attention of a specialist at a hospital.

Finally, the day of her examination arrived. Security procedures were set in motion. Cristina was handcuffed before leaving the prison, escorted under strict supervision, and transported by the official police vehicle. The moment Cristina arrived at the hospital, a police officer stuck close, almost like a shadow. It was clear—she wasn't just a patient; she was a prisoner. She waited for hours before her turn finally came, but every passing minute felt like a public spectacle. The weight of stares bore down on her, each gaze drawn to the cold metal of the handcuffs on her wrists.

Whispers floated through the air—some subtle, some not. It was as if she were some strange exhibits at a zoo, something to be observed and analyzed. Shame settled deep in her chest. The handcuffs weren't just restraints; they were a label, a sign that separated her from the rest of the world. When she was finally called in, the doctor informed her that no metallic objects were allowed during the examination. No one had warned her about this beforehand. The officer removed her handcuffs, but that wasn't her only problem—Cristina had ear piercings, and one of them had been in for so long that it had embedded itself into her skin. She swallowed her pride and asked for help. A doctor, a nurse—anyone. But her request was met with a cold, detached refusal. It wasn't a hospital procedure. Rules were rules.

A sympathetic nurse caught her eye, offering a silent acknowledgment that she could help. But before she could act, she was reminded—again—that policy came first. No help. No understanding. Just another moment that reinforced how alone Cristina truly was. I could be wrong, but I feel like in Brazil, hospital staff would have stepped in to fix a situation like this.

But no—after all the hassle of transportation, the endless waiting, and the sheer exhaustion, the whole examination was canceled over a tiny metal piercing. Seriously? Had she ever imagined, back when she first got that ear piercing, that something so small could lead to such a bizarre, humiliating ordeal?

Still handcuffed, ignored, and utterly powerless, Cristina was sent back to prison—without answers, without help. But strangely enough, what haunted her most wasn't the indifference of the medical staff. It was the deeper realization that, to the system, she was nothing. Just another body to be shuffled around, another task to be checked off someone's list. Not a person. Not someone worth understanding or caring about. And that—more than the missed examination, more than the ear piercing—was what truly hurt.

The harsh reality of prison life, combined with this experience, left a deep mark on her. It made it even harder for her to believe that anyone, anywhere, could truly understand—or even care.

Weeks later, I found myself at a hospital— for an emergency with my teenage daughter. As we rushed in, I noticed a young girl, probably around sixteen, sitting in handcuffs with a police officer standing beside her. At first glance, she looked indifferent, almost as if she wanted the world to believe she didn't care.

But I couldn't shake the feeling that, beneath that tough exterior, she was battling the same shame and pain that Cristina had once felt. I felt a deep sadness seeing her there. I silently prayed that, somehow, this moment would become a turning point for her—that she'd find inspiration instead of despair. But more than anything, I felt powerless.

How had we, as a society, allowed so many young people to end up in situations like this? Why weren't we doing more to prevent it?

Over time, I came to understand something about prison. It wasn't about fixing people or offering grand solutions. It was about presence. About showing up. In a place that often strips people of their humanity, even the smallest acts—a meaningful conversation, a moment of recognition, a reminder that someone still sees them—could plant the seed for change. And in that, I realized, was the true work: creating space for growth and reflection, one human connection at a time.

And so, little by little, I found my way. It wasn't always easy, but it was meaningful. As I adapted my approach, I began to see the potential for change—not just in the women I interacted with, but in myself too. This unexpected journey reshaped my perspective, deepening my understanding of both human nature and the power of a compassionate presence, even in the most challenging environments. This journey often led to incredible stories of personal growth—stories of resilience, of new intellectual passions being discovered within the prison walls.

I remember one conversation in particular. We were talking about what her life could look like after prison, brainstorming possibilities when she suddenly stopped talking and just stared into the air as if she were watching a movie of her past play out in front of her. Then, she sighed and said, "I was terrible at school. My grades were awful. I don't even know if I'd have a chance at a good university. A public university? Forget it. I probably couldn't even walk past one."

I looked at her and asked, "Do you really think school grades define intelligence?" That question changed the whole conversation. So, I started telling her about people who defied the odds—people whose intelligence and success had nothing to do with perfect report cards. "Take Abraham Lincoln," I said. "He barely had any formal schooling. His family moved around a lot, and they struggled financially. He had to work on the family farm instead of sitting in a classroom. But that didn't stop him. He taught himself to read and write using whatever books he could get his hands on. He was self-educated and determined. And, well, you know the rest of his story." Guess what? His sharp mind was the key to his success—not just anywhere, but as the President of the United States of America.

"And speaking of brilliant minds, remember Thomas Edison? Yep, the guy who lit up the world with the electric light bulb. More than 1,000 patents to his name! You'd think he was a genius in school, right? Nope. Edison struggled so much that his teachers thought he was slow and unable to keep up with the curriculum. And hey, did Mickey Mouse keep you company during your childhood? Fun fact: Walt Disney himself had a tough time in school, mostly because he couldn't focus in traditional classrooms. Sir Isaac Newton? One of the greatest scientific minds of all time? Believe it or not, he had a rough start too. As a kid, he was quiet, withdrawn, and even considered a poor student. His own mother nearly pulled him out of school to work on the family farm!"

She clapped her hands in excitement. "No way! You're kidding—tell me more, tell me more!" Alright, how about one of the most significant political figures of the 20th century...? Winston Churchill—one of the most significant political figures of the 20th century. The fearless Prime Minister who led the UK through

World War II. A man remembered for his powerful speeches and unshakable leadership. But what about his school days? Well, let's just say he wasn't exactly a star student. In fact, he failed the entrance exams for the Royal Military Academy. Twice. And you know what? Maybe that's the point. Maybe if people like Churchill had fit in perfectly at school, they wouldn't have become who they were meant to be. They'd be playing someone else's role, struggling to blend in instead of standing out.

Take Steve Jobs—our visionary, the mastermind behind Apple. He couldn't stand the rigid structure of traditional schooling. He wanted to follow his own curiosity, not just check off boxes on a syllabus. And look where that got him. So let it out! Let your creativity run wild! Forget the boxes they try to put you in—you've got a purpose, girl!"

She screamed with pure joy: "I do, I do, I do!" And me? I just stood there for a second, wondering—where the hell did all that inspiration even come from? Then I just smiled and silently thanked the angels. Sounds good, right?

Then I went home. I walked through the door, expecting the usual warm welcome, but instead, my daughter silently approached me. My heart sank. I could tell something was off. Uh-oh. Here comes some unsettling news. And there it was—she had gotten a bad grade on a school test.

Before I could even think, my brain launched into full-on critical parent mode. "You probably didn't study enough. If you spent less time on social media and paid more attention in class, maybe this wouldn't have happened..." The words rolled off my tongue before I could stop them. But something felt wrong. Even as I spoke, I could sense it. The disappointment on her face, the weight of my words—I knew, deep down, this wasn't the way to handle it. I paused mid-sentence. Had I gone too far? And then it hit me—none of this was going to change the fact that she got a bad grade.

It wasn't going to make her feel any better. And wasn't I supposed to be the one always preaching, "Marks don't define your worth!" and "Failure is just part of the journey!" Where was that wise, supportive voice now? Completely missing. Replaced by grumpy dad in full force.

I took a deep breath. As I looked at her, it hit me—she didn't need a lecture. She was already beating herself up just fine without my help. What she needed was a pep talk, not a TED Talk on Why Social Media is Ruining Your Life. So, I shifted gears. "Hey, I know you've got this. Everyone hits roadblocks, and this? This is just a steppingstone. You'll come out stronger—I know it."

She didn't exactly light up with joy, but I saw her shoulders relax just a little. And honestly? That felt like a win. No tears? I'll take it.

Later that night, as I replayed the day in my head, I had one of those oh wow moments. It's funny how hard it is to practice what you preach.

I've spent years talking about resilience, compassion, and how setbacks are just plot twists in our story. But the second my own daughter struggled, I defaulted to old-school tough love—like a parenting version of a bad dad joke. Unintentionally painful, but hey, at least there was a lesson in there somewhere.

Those prison visits, though—those were supposed to be the real lessons. I learned a lot from seeing people who had made big mistakes, and yet, I realized they were still human and deserving of empathy. It was a humbling experience that taught me to be more patient and forgiving. But when it came to my own kid? It turns out I needed a reminder to be that person I'm always telling others to be. So yeah, I messed up. But hey, that's life. You win some, you lose some, and sometimes, you just need to laugh at yourself.

I couldn't wait to tell Cristina about my little slip-up. If nothing else, it's proof that we're all still learning—even the so-called "wise" ones.

This might sound like a demagogical speech, but we really need to consider what defines us and who defines us. Considering the massive changes, we are undergoing formal studies are totally creativity-blocking, and creativity-limiting.

LEAVE THAT OLD LIFE BEHIND

We're living in a world full of massive uncertainties—recessions, inflation, political instability, rapid advancements in technology, pandemics, health crises, cyber threats, and stock market volatility. The list goes on. These uncertainties impact both our personal and professional lives. Will my job still exist in the future? What does "the future" even mean anymore? Should I invest time and money into learning something new? And if I do, will it even be relevant?

The key isn't about predicting the future—it's about turning uncertainty into an asset. The people who thrive won't be the ones who stick rigidly to a pre-planned path—like getting a specific degree or following a set career trajectory. Instead, success will belong to those who can adapt, learn, and reinvent themselves as the world changes. It's easy to spiral into fear when facing uncertainty. But fear requires no effort—it comes naturally. The same goes for judgment. Society will always have opinions, and often, they won't be kind. Whether it's fear of professional failure or personal setbacks, judgment feels inescapable.

That's where I have to think of Jesus and the Stone Throwing situation—John 8:2-11. Who is truly in a position to judge anyone else? Instead of being consumed by fear or criticism, what if we focused on growth, adaptability, and resilience? So, picture this: It's early morning, and Jesus is back at the temple, casually teaching a crowd of people. Everyone's hanging onto his words when suddenly, a group of religious leaders—the Pharisees and teachers of the law—storm in, dragging a woman with them. "Teacher!" they announce, full of self-righteous energy. "This woman was caught red-handed in adultery. And according to Moses' law, she should be stoned. What do you say?" Now, they weren't really looking for wisdom; they were trying to trap Jesus. If he said, "Let her go," they'd accuse him of ignoring the law. If he said, "Stone her," well, that would go against his whole message of grace.

But Jesus? Oh, he was way ahead of them. Instead of answering right away, he just bent down and started writing in the dirt. (What was he writing? No one knows, but I like to think it was something cheeky.) The Pharisees kept pushing, demanding an answer. Finally, Jesus stood up, looked them in the eye, and said, "Alright, whichever one of you has never sinned, go ahead—be the first to throw a stone."

Mic drop.

Then he went back to doodling in the dirt. One by one, the accusers realized they were caught in their own hypocrisy. The older ones left first (maybe because they had more years of mistakes to reflect on), and eventually, it was just Jesus and the woman. Jesus stood up and smiled at her. "Where'd everyone go? Has no one condemned you?" "No one, sir," she said, probably still in shock. "Then I don't condemn you either," Jesus replied. "Now go on—leave that old life behind."

The point is, we're all in the same boat. Life's challenges affect us all. So why do some people take advantage of others or hold grudges in the face of someone else's misfortune? Shouldn't hardship teach us compassion instead of cruelty?

Take pharmacies during the COVID-19 pandemic. You'd think they'd be all about helping people, right? Well, not always. Reports surfaced of some pharmacies and healthcare providers price-gouging essential supplies—masks, sanitizers, you name it. And it didn't stop there. Some shady players were caught up in fraudulent billing, charging for COVID-19 tests and vaccines that never even happened.

Talk about cashing in on a crisis. Then there's Volkswagen's infamous "Dieselgate" scandal. Some geniuses over there decided it'd be a great idea to install sneaky software in their diesel cars to cheat emissions tests. Basically, the car would play nice during testing, making regulators think it was eco-friendly. But out on the road? It was spewing out pollutants like nobody's business—way beyond legal limits. And let's not forget the opioid crisis. This one's downright tragic. Some large corporations allegedly bribed pharmacy benefit managers to keep opioids flowing freely fueling an epidemic that led to thousands of overdose deaths of innocent people. All in the name of profit.

Now, if we look at these cases through a pragmatic lens, we might call it "unscrupulous innovation." But let's be real—it's just unethical business. That creativity could have been used for something else, for something noble. So as Jesus said, let us go on—leave that old life behind, and start something new and good for all.

The Glass is Half Full or Half Empty?

Not every innovation is a good one—let's be honest. But what if we could channel our skills, our creativity, and even our past mistakes toward something meaningful? Imagine if those who had taken the wrong path before—no matter what kind of misstep—could step up as guiding lights, helping others avoid the same pitfalls. No shame, no fear of judgment. Just openness, honesty, and a commitment to doing better. Take Lina, for example. She was stuck in a rut—unmotivated, uninterested, just going through the motions.

Every time we talked, she'd sigh and tell me she just wasn't in the mood to learn German. And honestly? I got it. Even though the prison offered free classes, even though she knew learning the language could help her future, she just couldn't push herself to start. She called it her inner Hund—her inner resistance, as they say in Germany. The social worker teaching the class tried everything to encourage her. She painted pictures of future opportunities, of how speaking German could open doors for Lina. But nothing clicked. And over time, I learned something: you can't force change. When people aren't ready, pushing too hard can do more harm than good. Sometimes, the best thing you can do is wait. Wait for that moment when they're open when they're ready to hear the message—and then be there to guide them forward.

So, I decided to take a different approach. Instead of pushing, I sparked a conversation about two mindsets I believe live in all of us. I told Lina, "There's a part of your mind that's wired to focus on problems and another part that looks for opportunities."

Some people think these are just two different kinds of people—pessimists vs. optimists. But I don't buy that. I think we all have both sides; the real question is, which one do we listen to? If you train your mind to see problems, guess what? It'll get really good at justifying them. Every setback, every obstacle, every little inconvenience becomes proof that things won't work out. But if you train your mind to see opportunities, a different story starts to take shape. You'll notice possibilities, focus on potential rewards, and convince yourself that the effort is worth it.

I didn't expect Lina to have some overnight epiphany. But I did see a shift—a small one, but a shift nonetheless. The seed had been planted. To drive the point home, I shared a story from my own life. Back when I was finishing my bachelor's degree, I saw a simple, old-school notice on the university bulletin board. It was for a 12-month internship at a chemical company, with a shot at a full-time contract afterward. Interesting, I thought. But there was a catch—actually, a few. A friend of mine was also eyeing the position, and honestly, she had a better chance. She spoke fluent German; I barely knew a handful of phrases. We weighed the pros and cons together, and we both hesitated. The commute was brutal—poor bus connections, never-ending traffic, and it meant waking up at 4:30 AM every day.

At that moment, we had a choice: focus on the problems or the possibilities. I didn't mind the challenges. Instead, I started picturing the possibilities: a well-paid job, a stronger resume, and maybe even buying a car and traveling to Germany. The early mornings and long commutes? Just temporary obstacles.

My friend, on the other hand, saw things differently. She couldn't get past the thought of waking up at 4 AM, cramming onto crowded buses, and spending two hours stuck in traffic every day. We went back and forth for hours, looking at the situation from both perspectives— opportunity vs. problem. In the end, I applied for the job. She didn't. Instead, she found a position much closer to home. It was convenient, sure—but it was also a small company with little room to grow.

As for me? I got the job. After 12 months, they offered me a permanent contract, and soon enough, I bought my first car. Then, three years later, the company moved to a beautiful, well-developed town in the São Paulo countryside—talk about a jackpot. I relocated with them, and a few years later, they sent me to work in their research and development labs in the USA. That's where I met my husband, and eventually, we moved to Germany to work at the company's headquarters. Meanwhile, my friend stayed in her comfort zone. She hopped between small companies, some of which went bankrupt, while others struggled to pay fair wages. A few years ago, I heard she was unemployed, desperately searching for a new job.

This wake-up call isn't about comparing outcomes. It's not about deciding whose fate was better or worse— it's about the journey, and the lessons we gain through our choices and goal-setting. When we approach life with a positive mindset—focused on opportunities—it's almost like we send a signal to the Universe. Suddenly, things start falling into place. The right people show up at just the right time, in just the right way, to help us move forward.

The path ahead won't always be clear, but by choosing to see possibilities instead of roadblocks, we open ourselves up to unexpected opportunities—ones that might challenge us, surprise us, and push us to grow in ways we never imagined. But when we fixate on obstacles? That's when we get stuck. We focus on what we lack, what could go wrong, and all the reasons something won't work. And here's the thing: this mindset doesn't just slow us down—it actually closes doors before we even try to walk through them. We start seeing the world through a filter of limitations, convincing ourselves that the challenges are bigger than the solutions. But are they?

More often than not, the obstacles we fear aren't as impossible as they seem. The key is in how we choose to see them. When we start viewing challenges as steppingstones instead of stop signs, we unlock a whole new way of thinking—and that's where real growth begins. The truth is, that how we see things shapes how we experience them. When we approach life with a mindset that seeks solutions and embraces the journey, the process itself becomes just as valuable—if not more—than the final outcome.

There's no "one-size-fits-all" formula for success. But one thing is certain: our approach defines the kind of experiences we create along the way. Opportunities don't always show up in the way we expect, but if we stay open to them, they will come. Often, the biggest breakthroughs don't happen at the finish line—they happen in the small moments, in the unexpected connections, in the twists and turns that shape us as we move toward our goals.

So, what if every challenge you face is actually a steppingstone? What if every detour, every setback, every frustrating "no" is a nudge in the right direction—helping you refine your purpose, strengthening your resilience, and deepening your understanding of what truly matters? Would you still see obstacles? Or would you start seeing opportunities where others only see roadblocks? The way we view the journey shapes not only our success but our entire experience of life. It's up to us to decide what kind of experience we want to create. And let's be real—getting stuck in the "should have" loop isn't helping anyone. How many times have you replayed those mind-movie scenes of regret? "I should have done this." "I should have chosen that." Sound familiar?

Here's the problem: this kind of thinking doesn't change the past—it just gives it more power. It drains your energy, keeping you trapped in old narratives instead of moving forward. The more time you spend dwelling on what you could have changed, the more you reinforce the very things you wish you had avoided. So why not flip the script? Instead of feeding the past, focus on what you can shape now. That's where your real power is. It's important to focus on the opportunities in front of you—not the obstacles, no matter what form they take, whether from the past or the present.

We don't want to keep reliving or perpetuating old "mistakes." The past is gone. It has no power over us—unless we give it power. The key is to shift our mindset: to embrace the lessons we've learned without letting them anchor us in regret. Every new moment is a chance to rewrite our story, to step forward, and, if we're open to it, to experience something holy.

As I shared this story with Lina, I could see something shift in her expression. She nodded, realizing that she, too, had once seen opportunities where others only saw obstacles. We talked about people who spend hours in line just to get the latest iPhone. Why do they do it? Because they're focused on the reward, not the discomfort of standing in a long line. Then, we flipped the perspective: What about times we've clung to relationships that only caused suffering—just because we convinced ourselves there was still an opportunity where, in reality, there was none?

Then, at just the right moment, I brought the conversation back to learning German. "So, tell me," I asked Lina, "do you see learning German as an obstacle or an opportunity?" She hesitated.

I could almost see the gears turning in her mind. And then, something clicked. "True," she said, almost surprised at herself. "I'm definitely focusing on the obstacle here. I haven't even let myself dream about the opportunities it could bring." And just like that, her imagination took off. She started spinning ideas—what if she could give private German classes? What if she could become a translator? What if this one skill opened doors for her career in marketing? The possibilities were endless. She knew what to do next. And, most importantly, she found her own motivation—not through pressure, but by shifting her focus from the obstacle to the reward. Because the best mentors don't just teach skills. They help break through self-limiting beliefs.

Lina was smart—she threw the ball right back into my court. "But haven't you ever had a moment where you felt absolutely terrified? Like, convinced you were going to fail, and everyone would see you as a total loser?" she asked, almost as if she needed one final push to jump over her self-made obstacle.

I took a deep breath. It's always easier to spot weaknesses in someone else's thinking than to face your own. I scanned my memory for a moment she could really relate to—something a little silly, maybe even funny, but that had once felt like a full-blown monster in my mind. And then, the perfect example hit me: our first family ski vacation.

I grew up in São Paulo, where snow isn't exactly a thing. The first time I ever saw snow was when I was about 25, during a trip to Quebec. So, naturally, I had never learned to ski—and, to be honest, I had never really wanted to. But my kids? Oh, they really wanted to ski. At the time, they were 13 and 10 years old, and thanks to their mother's total lack of interest in winter sports, they had barely ever set foot on a slope. I knew I couldn't let my resistance become their limitation. So, I took up the challenge.

When we got to the ski resort, I stood there watching little kids—some barely 3 years old—glide effortlessly down the slopes. I mean, these tiny humans were sucking their thumbs while skiing. Skiing! Meanwhile, their parents skied ahead, completely confident that their kids would just follow along. And you know what? The kids did. No fear, no overthinking, no comparing themselves to others. They just experienced the process, trusted the guidance, and went for it. And there I was, a fully grown adult, completely frozen—not because of the cold, but because of my own mind.

At first, I thought, well, obviously, these kids must live here. They probably ski every weekend. That's why they look like they were born with skis on their feet. But no. I started paying closer attention to the little ones who were just learning. At first, they had no more balance than an adult trying skiing for the first time. They fell. They cried. But here's the thing—30 minutes later, I looked again, and they were no longer falling. Instead, they were wobbling back and forth, experimenting, figuring it out.

By the end of the day, they were already riding up the mountain with their little ski school friends, zooming down the slopes as if they'd always known how to do it. And then came Sunday. My first ski lesson. It was a totally last-minute decision—I wasn't even sure if I was going to do it. There wasn't a group class at my level, which meant I had to take a private lesson. Ugh. I wasn't exactly thrilled about the idea. Learning to ski at 48 years old? The thought alone made me want to roll myself into a warm blanket and stay in the lodge with a hot chocolate. But I went for it.

The lesson lasted two hours. I learned the basics: how to put on and take off the skis (harder than it sounds), move uphill, slide downhill, turn, and, most importantly, not land flat on my face. Trying to ski down even the tiniest incline felt like balancing on a pair of greased-up toothpicks. And don't even get me started on the ski boots—walking in those things should have been a separate course on its own! An hour passed, and my instructor suddenly announced, "Okay, now we're going to climb the mountain!" I blinked. Excuse me? "No, no, I need to practice more!" I protested. He just grinned. "We're going to practice by skiing down the mountain." Oh. Fantastic.

So, up we went using the T-bar lift. If you've never used one, let me paint a picture: It's this pole with a little bar at the end that you stick between your legs while it drags you uphill. Sounds easy? It's not. You do not sit on it—you just lean, holding on for dear life while trying not to lose balance. It takes arm and leg strength, and guess what? I had neither at that moment.

Halfway up, disaster struck. I wobbled, lost my balance, and—boom—down I went, right in the steepest part of the incline. I panicked. My instructor, staying as calm as a monk, simply said, "Alright, we'll ski down from here." Ski down? At that angle? With what skills, sir? I was sweating bullets.

He handed me one end of his ski pole, held the other, and we inched our way down, stopping every few meters while he corrected my stance. What felt like a death-defying descent was, in reality, probably no more than a one-kilometer slope.

By the time we reached the bottom (about an hour later), my legs were jelly, my heart was racing, and my dignity? Let's just say I left that somewhere on the mountainside. Just as I was catching my breath, my kids came running over, excited. "Mom! How was the lesson?"

I looked at them, still processing the trauma, and gave the most honest answer I could. "Well... I survived. I think it was my first and last time," I added.

That evening, as I sat with my sore muscles and bruised pride, my youngest son looked up at me with big, hopeful eyes and said, "Mom, don't give up. I really want to ski with you." That did it. That one sentence lit a spark in me. Suddenly, I didn't just want to ski—I needed to. Not just for me, but for us. That night, I meditated. I closed my eyes, took a deep breath, and mentally reached out to the Collective Knowledge.

I asked, "There must be an easier way to experience this. What am I not understanding?" And then it hit me. I had been putting all my trust in scarcity—in what I lacked. I wasn't trusting in the abundance that was already there, the natural flow of learning, the way kids embrace new experiences without overthinking. Instead, I had tuned into the frequency of fear, of Ego— the voice that says, You can't. You're too old. You'll fail.

But fear is a trickster. When we stand too close to it, it warps reality. The key isn't to fight fear but to step back and observe it from a distance. When we do that, we realize something profound: fear is just a construct of the mind. It only has the power we give it. In that moment of clarity, I remembered something important—we are not just bodies struggling through challenges; we are Spirit, limitless, and capable. The body is neutral—it simply follows the script our mind writes for it. If we tell it we're weak, it obeys. If we tell it we're strong, it listens. I had been looking for strength in the wrong place. Strength doesn't come from resisting fear—it comes from stepping outside of it. And just like that, I knew. Tomorrow, I'd get back on those skis. And this time, I wouldn't fight the process. I'd flow with it.

That night, I decided to visualize the experience exactly the way I wanted it to unfold. First, I meditated—not just for myself, but with my ski instructor in mind. I had read that early in the morning when our minds are still in the theta state, subconscious communication is stronger. Why not try? I imagined him standing in front of me, and the words flowed naturally. "I'm sorry for not trusting you. For putting my faith in my own scarcity instead of in the abundance you were offering me."

Then, I shifted my mindset. I chose to believe that I already knew how to ski. I set a clear goal: I want to ski down the long slopes with my family. I reminded myself that if fear arose, I would stay focused on my goal, not the discomfort. I reflected on a truth deeply ingrained in Kriya Yoga—staying in the Spirit, in the purpose. This same wisdom echoes throughout the Bible, expressed in different words but carrying the same essence: "The Lord is always in my presence; with Him by my side, I shall not be shaken." (Psalm 16:8)

The next morning, my instructor arrived and said, "We're going to climb the mountain now." I hesitated. "No, I think I should practice more first." He smiled and simply said, "Trust me." What could I say? Did I really have an option? Giving up was not my option at that moment.

We went up. I was alone on one T-bar, and my instructor was right behind me on another. Fear crept in. My hands were sweating. Stay in the goal. I repeated to myself. And then—I didn't fall off the T-bar! That alone felt like a victory after my embarrassing tumble the day before. When we reached the top of the mountain, I managed to detach from the bar and ski away without falling! My instructor arrived right behind me, and when he saw I'd done it, he erupted with joy. He hugged me and shouted, "You did it! You did it!"

Before we began the descent, he started explaining how we'd ski down. Then he paused, looking thoughtful, and started saying some of the very phrases I had spoken to him during my meditation. I couldn't believe it. This is real. We're synchronized. Quantum physics talks about this kind of connection—I had read about it, but now I was living it.

The descent was still challenging, but something had shifted. My confidence grew. The fear was still there, but now, the possibility was there too. By the third day, I skied with my family on the long slope. By the fourth day, we skied twice down even longer, steeper inclines. I couldn't believe it. Neither could my family. Lina was captivated. She could feel my story—my struggle, my fear, my breakthrough. She could relate. And in that moment, we connected.

MARKETING AND COMMUNICATION EXCHANGE TIME

Adriana had spent three years in prison, and now she was ready to plan her comeback. Back home, she had built a thriving little communications agency with a loyal base of recurring clients. From supermarkets to bakeries and fashion stores, her business was at some point on the rise.

But then, things started slipping. Clients left. Motivation dipped. The challenges piled up, and for the first time, she felt like she was losing control. Adriana hit a low and the rest is story. But instead of bottling everything up, she finally opened up about her struggles—and, surprisingly, about what she planned to do once she got past this rough patch.

It was the first time she really reflected on where things had gone wrong and what she wanted next. She was determined to reclaim her business and asked me to help her brainstorm a way forward. Of course, I was all in.

We started breaking things down together, beginning with her business's competitive advantages. What made her agency special? Why did clients come to her in the first place? Right away, two things stood out: flexibility and a hands-on, personalized approach. Unlike the big, bureaucratic agencies, Adriana's business was nimble. She could pivot quickly, adapt to changes, and respond to client needs faster than the big players. That kind of agility was a serious advantage. On top of that, her personal touch set her apart. Clients didn't feel like just another number—they got tailor-made solutions, not cookie-cutter strategies. And that? That was a game-changer.

Another major strength we uncovered. Adriana's deep local expertise. This wasn't just a nice-to-have—it was unique. She knew the ins and outs of the local market, which meant she wasn't just throwing out generic marketing strategies. She created campaigns that actually resonated with her audience because she understood the cultural and social nuances that big agencies often overlooked. Clients didn't just see her as another service provider; they saw her as a trusted partner who truly got them. But of course, no business is without its weak spots. And when we shifted gears to talk about her competitive disadvantages, Adriana didn't hesitate—she knew exactly where she needed to improve.

One of her biggest challenges? Over-promising and under-delivering. Creativity was one of her biggest strengths, but sometimes, in the excitement of pitching new ideas, she'd promise more than she could realistically pull off. That was a dangerous game. When unexpected costs—like last-minute design changes or unplanned communication materials—popped up, her budget would spiral out of control. And when costs went up, profits shrank. It wasn't just about money, either.

Over-promising puts a strain on client relationships. Expectations were sky-high, and when she couldn't meet them, trust took a hit. Another weak spot? Adriana hadn't reinvested enough in technology. While competitors were using automation tools, AI, and advanced analytics to streamline their workflows and optimize campaigns, she was still doing things the old-school way. And in a fast-moving industry, that was a problem. Without the right tech, her business wasn't scaling as efficiently as it could. She couldn't track campaign performance in real-time, automate repetitive tasks, or predict customer behavior with the accuracy that cutting-edge tools allowed. In short, she was working harder not smarter.

It actually reminded me of what happened to Blackberry. Remember when Blackberry was in the smartphone industry? They had a lock on the business world—secure emails, those iconic keyboards, and a reputation for being the device for professionals. But then? They got comfortable. While Apple and Samsung were revolutionizing the game with sleek touchscreens and an app-driven ecosystem, Blackberry stuck to their old model, convinced people would never let go of physical keyboards. Spoiler alert: They did.

The same thing happened with Nokia. They ruled the mobile world at one point, but when smartphones started shifting towards software-driven innovation, Nokia clung to their hardware-first mindset. Meanwhile, Apple and Android brands ran circles around them with cutting-edge operating systems and endless possibilities.

The lesson? Businesses that don't evolve get left behind. And Adriana's lack of investment in technology wasn't just a minor inconvenience—it was holding her back from staying competitive in an industry where speed, efficiency, and data-driven decisions were everything. And that brings us to a bigger truth: competitive advantage is never permanent.

It's not something you win once and keep forever—it's a constant game of adaptation and reinvention. Back to our examples, at one point, Nokia owned the mobile phone market. If you didn't have a Nokia, were you even texting? But then the industry started shifting. Smartphones weren't just about hardware anymore; they were about software, apps, and seamless user experiences. They stuck to what they knew instead of evolving with the times. It wasn't just one bad decision that took them down—it was a series of missteps. Maybe their executives felt too secure in their dominance. Maybe they underestimated how quickly consumer preferences were changing.

Either way, while Apple and Android brands were innovating like crazy, Nokia lagged behind. They missed the shift toward smartphones and the whole ecosystem-based approach that Apple mastered. And in business, if you don't move fast enough, you get left behind. The lesson? No matter how strong your advantage is today, it won't last unless you actively work to maintain and evolve it.

Reflecting on Nokia's story was a wake-up call for Adriana. She realized that even though her competitive advantage was strong right now, it wouldn't stay that way unless she actively worked to improve it. She couldn't just rely on what had worked in the past—she needed to double down on agility, sharpen her innovation, and, most importantly, break the habit of over-promising and under-delivering.

She also saw the bigger picture: technology wasn't just a "nice to have" anymore—it was a necessity. If she wanted her business to be more efficient, scalable, and competitive, she had to start reinvesting in the right tools and systems. By the end of our conversation, something had shifted in her. That spark? It was back.

For the first time in a long time, she wasn't just thinking about survival—she was thinking about winning. She was ready. Ready to take back control of her business. Ready to make a comeback. Ready to prove—to herself more than anyone—that this time, things would be different. This time, she wouldn't create obstacles for herself. She'd embrace opportunities.

Because success? It wasn't just about quick wins. It was about adapting, evolving, and staying in the game for the long haul.

WHEN THE BEST WORDS ARE SAID IN SILENCE

Sometimes, when I meet the girls in prison, words just aren't needed. They don't feel like talking. Instead, the emotions spill out in silent tears, and in those moments, all they want is a hug—no judgment, no rushed advice, no empty words that won't change a thing. And if that's what they need, that's exactly what I give them.

But sometimes, they push through that wave of emotion and look for something more—a word of encouragement, a reminder that hope still exists. When that happens, I offer what I can. Maybe it's a quiet prayer. Maybe it's a song, our voices blending together in a shared moment of release, of connection, of hope. Because in those moments, it's not about fixing anything. It's about being there.

Speaking of songs, there's one that has become a staple in my time with the girls—*Take Me Home,*

Country Roads by John Denver. For those who speak English, it's almost like a ritual.

The moment the first few words are sung, voices start joining in, one by one, until we're all singing together: "Country roads, take me home, to the place I belong West Virginia, mountain mama take me home, country roads..." The lyrics hit differently in here. That longing for home, for belonging—it's something we all feel in one way or another. And when we sing, for just a moment, the walls around us fade, and we're somewhere else. Somewhere free.

This song, in its simplicity, is more than just a tune. West Virginia isn't just a place—it's a metaphor. It represents anywhere that tugs at your soul, that deep sense of belonging. Sometimes, it's a place you've never even been. Other times, it's somewhere you thought you had forgotten. Or maybe it's the echoes of a childhood memory, distant but never really gone.

For the girls, singing is more than just passing the time. It's a way to express longing—for connection, for a home that feels safe, for something warm and familiar. It's also, for some, a way to grieve the home they once had but lost, even if only for a moment.

Another song they love—especially when searching for comfort or deeper meaning—is the Brazilian classic *O Que É, O Que É* by Gonzaguinha. The lyrics aren't just words; they're a reflection on life itself—its mysteries, contradictions, and fleeting nature: "And life...What is life? Tell me, my brother, Is it the beat of a heart? Is it a sweet illusion? "And life...Is it a marvel or suffering? Is it joy or lament? What is it, what is it, my brother?"

Some say life is nothing more than a passing moment—a drop in the ocean, gone in an instant. And yet, even in that brief flicker, there is meaning. There is hope. This song is more than just lyrics and melody—it's an invitation to wrestle with the complexities of existence. It acknowledges life's fleeting nature while reminding us that, even in its brevity, there is meaning. There is a struggle, but there is also beauty. And for the girls, it becomes a quiet moment of recognition—a way to accept that life can be hard, yet still hold space for joy, even in the smallest of moments.

When they get lost in the spiral of their thoughts, when their minds are racing but they don't even realize they need peace, I try to meet them where they are. Sometimes, I offer words of comfort. For those who come from Christian backgrounds, I share passages that speak to their hearts—verses that remind them they are not alone, and that peace is still within reach.

Three bible passages, in particular, always resonate deeply. In Luke 2:14, when Jesus is born, the angels proclaim to the shepherds: "Glory to God in the highest, and on earth peace, goodwill toward men!" Or in John 14:27, Jesus Himself offers these reassuring words: "Peace I leave with you; the peace I give to you. I do not give to you as the world gives. Let not your heart be troubled, neither let it be afraid."

Sometimes I remind them to appeal to the "highest court" remembering the passage in Philippians 4:6–7: "Do not be anxious about anything, but in every situation, by prayer and petition, with thanksgiving, present your requests to God. And the peace of God, which transcends all understanding, will guard your hearts and your minds in Christ Jesus." In moments of doubt, of sorrow, of restless searching—these words become an anchor. A reminder that even in the chaos, peace is still possible. These aren't just words; they are invitations—a call to claim what is already ours. Peace isn't something we have to chase in the outside world.

It's not something we have to earn. It's already within us, waiting to be recognized and embraced. It's a gift we are all entitled to—if only we are willing to reach for it.

Depending on their beliefs, we might also delve into Spiritism as taught by Allan Kardec.

Another powerful source of wisdom I often turn to—one that has helped me countless times—is *A Course in Miracles*. One lesson, in particular, always stands out: "The mind which means that all it wants is peace must join with other minds, for that is how peace is obtained. And when the wish for peace is genuine, the means for finding it is given, in a form each mind that seeks for it in honesty can understand." (W-185.6:1-4)

What strikes me most about this is that peace isn't just an individual pursuit—it's found in connection, in understanding, in the moments where our hearts and minds truly meet. But there's a catch. Peace isn't just about asking—it's about giving it, too. That sounds obvious, but it's anything but easy.

How many times do we convince ourselves that someone else—or some external situation—is the reason we don't have peace? As if peace were something that could be taken from us. As if we had no choice at all. But the truth is, peace is an inside job. And the moment we stop outsourcing it to others, we begin to set ourselves free.

It's easy to feel at peace when everything is falling into place—when work is steady, relationships are strong, and life feels predictable. But the real test of peace isn't in the easy moments. It's in the storms. It's when challenges arise, when uncertainty creeps in, when obstacles feel overwhelming. That's when peace feels distant. That's when our perception shifts, and we start believing that it has been taken from us. But the truth is, we can't give peace to others if we don't have it within ourselves first. And to give, we must first receive.

You know, one of my go-to methods for connecting with the girls in prison is storytelling. There's something about a well-told story that reaches people in ways that pure logic and reasoning just can't. Some lessons, especially the deeper ones about life, need to be felt rather than explained. That's where I often turn to Yoga and Buddhist teachings.

One of the most powerful spiritual texts I rely on is the Bhagavad Gita. It beautifully illustrates the struggles we face—the battles within our own minds—

and offers profound wisdom on how to navigate them. But if I had to pick a favorite, it would be the story of Narada and the Illusion of Maya. It goes like this: "Narada, a celestial sage and devoted follower of Lord Vishnu, was curious. One day, he approached Vishnu and asked, "O Lord, I've heard so much about Maya. But what exactly is it?" Vishnu smiled knowingly. "You'll understand soon, Narada," he said. "But first, do me a favor—fetch me some water from the river." Narada, being ever obedient, went to the river. But just as he bent down to fill his pot, something happened—he saw a woman. A beautiful woman. The moment their eyes met, he was completely captivated. In that instant, he forgot everything—Vishnu, the water, even his spiritual quest."

We see here how fast our minds get distracted from what really matters. Fast forward—"Narada and the woman fell in love, got married, and built a life together. They had children, he worked hard, struggled, celebrated victories, endured heartbreaks—he lived it all. Then one day, disaster struck. A terrible flood came and swept away everything—his home, his wife, his children. Narada, drowning in despair, cried out for help. And just like that, Vishnu appeared. With a gentle smile, he asked, "Narada… where is my water?" In that moment, everything Narada had lived through—his entire life—vanished. It had all been an illusion."

Now, I know I may not be doing full justice to this story, but trust me, if you really want to feel it the way it's meant to be told, go watch Murali Venkatrao, the master storyteller from Bangalore. The way he narrates, you won't just hear the story—you'll live it. It's an experience you don't want to miss. But back to our goal, peace. If we let trouble steal our peace, then we won't find peace in the trouble.

But if we learn to quiet the noise, to listen beyond the storm, we might just hear the whisper that was there all along. Choosing peace isn't always easy—especially when fear and uncertainty feel overwhelming. But the truth is, peace is always available. It's a shift in perception, a choice we make. We can stay trapped in the chaos of fear, letting it dictate our reality. Or we can step back, re-center ourselves, and choose peace. And like any practice, the more we choose it, the more natural it becomes. The more we cultivate it within ourselves, the more we can offer it to others.

I am incredibly fortunate that my time with the girls in prison gives me countless opportunities to remind myself of this practice. Their stories are more than just testaments to resilience—they challenge everything we think we know about people, about transformation, about what it truly means to awaken. If we keep an open and still mind, we might just discover that even in the most difficult circumstances, the most illuminating insights can emerge. May all beings everywhere be happy and free.

Acknowledgement

This book would not have been possible without the support, encouragement, and inspiration of so many incredible individuals. First and foremost, I extend my deepest gratitude to the women I have met in prison. Their stories, resilience, and willingness to share their experiences have profoundly shaped my understanding of humanity and compassion. Without their openness, this book would have no foundation.

I am also deeply grateful to my family, who have stood by me throughout this journey, even when they didn't fully understand my motivation. Their patience, love, and unwavering belief in me have been my anchor. A special thank you to my husband, Konrad, and my children, André, Julia, and Matheo—you are my greatest source of strength and joy. To my friends and colleagues, thank you for the thought-provoking conversations, the moments of reflection, and the encouragement to keep writing. A special thank you to Débora, and Mariana, as well as the Course in Miracles crew, Krina and Oli—your wisdom and support have been invaluable. A special thank you also goes to those who work within the prison system—the staff, volunteers, and advocates who dedicate themselves to making a difference in the lives of incarcerated individuals. Their commitment to rehabilitation, education, and human dignity is a powerful reminder that compassion can thrive in even the most unexpected places.

Finally, I want to acknowledge you, the reader. Whether you picked up this book out of curiosity, personal experience, or a desire to see the world from a different perspective, I appreciate your willingness to engage with these stories. May they challenge us, inspire us, and deepen our understanding of the unseen lives behind prison walls but above all of our own imaginary prison walls.

With gratitude,

Marisa Cruz

About The Author

Marisa Cruz is not a bestselling author—at least, not yet. This is her first published book, born from a deep passion for peace, compassion, and the power of human connection. When she's not volunteering in different ways, you'll find her dreaming about her next adventure abroad. She loves hiking, meditating, and traveling—always seeking new places that inspire her. Marisa currently lives with her family near Frankfurt, Germany, where she continues to believe in—and dream of—a little piece of heaven on earth.